The Still Small Voice

A BOOK FOR BUSY PEOPLE

The Still Small Voice

A BOOK FOR BUSY PEOPLE

Readings © the individual contributors
Compilation © 2012 Neil Paynter
First published 2012 by
Wild Goose Publications, Fourth Floor, Savoy House,
140 Sauchiehall Street, Glasgow G2 3DH, UK,
the publishing division of the Iona Community. Scottish Charity No. SC003794.
Limited Company Reg. No. SC096243.

ISBN 978-1-84952-242-7

Overseas distribution
Australia: Willow Connection Pty Ltd, Unit 4A, 3–9 Kenneth Road,
Manly Vale, NSW 2093
New Zealand: Pleroma, Higginson Street, Otane 4170, Central Hawkes Bay
Canada: Bayard Distribution, 10 Lower Spadina Ave., Suite 400, Toronto,
Ontario M5V 2Z

Printed by Bell & Bain, Thornliebank, Glasgow

And he said, Go forth, and stand upon the mount before the Lord. And, behold, the Lord passed by, and a great and strong wind rent the mountains, and brake in pieces the rocks before the Lord; but the Lord was not in the wind: and after the wind an earthquake; but the Lord was not in the earthquake: And after the earthquake a fire; but the Lord was not in the fire: and after the fire a still small voice.

1 Kings 19:11–12 (KJV)

The human voice can never reach the distance that is covered by the still small voice of conscience.

Mahatma Gandhi

Introduction

I don't know about you but I find life just seems to be getting busier and busier. And even when I'm not 'doing' my poor mind seems eternally *busy*. Life seems so full of distractions, different messages: babble ...

So: a book of daily readings to help folk still themselves ...

I've used some of these pieces myself in my daily discipline as a member of the Iona Community. The readings are short – sometimes very short – because sometimes it feels like there are enough words in the world! The world is so crowded with words it makes it difficult to focus on the Word.

The Still Small Voice is a book for those who feel themselves travelling at an increasingly frantic pace each day, and are hungry for snatches of nourishment to feed their souls – energy and inspiration and wonder to help keep them on the Way.

Jesus lived a balanced life of reflection and action, of times rooted in prayer and contemplation and of times engaged in the tangled messy thick of it. This is a little book to help with that balance.

In *Hard Words for Interesting Times* (Wild Goose Publications) John Bell writes: *And what does Elijah hear in that silence? Is it a voice which says, 'You are my beloved son in whom I am well pleased?' No. It is a voice that seems to be singularly unimpressed with Elijah's show of piety. It is a voice that says, 'Go back into the city which you are running away from. I have work for you there.'*

A good quote to begin with; and to end.

Peace,

Neil Paynter,
Ordinary Time, 2012

> *God, help us to hear your voice*
> *through the babble of this busy world*
> *where words are used to confuse,*
> *distract,*
> *manipulate,*
> *sell illusion,*
> *buy power;*
> *help us to be still and receptive to your healing,*
> *encouraging,*
> *inspiring,*
> *enduring,*
> *life-giving Word.*

January 1

The Solemnity of Mary, Mother of God

Mary, earthy mother,
common woman:
you sing to your son
songs that will move hearts
to change the world, if only
we learn to listen
and delve to the deep
human source
of your heavenly music.

Joy Mead, from *A Telling Place*

January 2

God of all new beginnings,
thank you for the promise of the journey.

Tom Gordon, from *A Blessing to Follow*

January 3

Help me to see the connections
welcome the intertwinings
let go the pain and embrace the future.

Kate McIlhagga, from *The Green Heart of the Snowdrop*

January 4

God
in my good days and bad days
help me
to hear you affirm
your delight in me.

Beckon me into your joy.

Ruth Burgess, from *Friends and Enemies*

January 5

God, teach us to value the here and now,
because this is all we ever have,
this is what is most real,
and this, this here and now,
is our starting point.

Brian Woodcock, from *Around a Thin Place*

January 6

Epiphany

Jesus,
may we not hoard,
but freely give
the gold of our hearts,

January

the myrrh of our grief,
the frankincense of our dreams
to You.

Mary Palmer, from *Hay and Stardust*

January 7

'Pray for more light, and follow the light that you see'
was an early motto of the Iona Community.

From *George MacLeod: A Biography*

January 8

God, you make each one of us a little different from the others.
You make each of us special in some way.
Help us learn from each other and
with each other this year,
so that we discover the gifts
you give us in each other.

Nancy Cocks, from *Growing up with God*

January 9

To begin and end the day in prayer is to wrap the day in sanctity – all
events and encounters within that time are then encompassed in God's
care.

Annie Heppenstall, from *Wild Goose Chase*

January 10

Help us to be, to listen in the waiting
for the still small voice
which speaks of promises unbroken
beneath our doubt and fear and forgetting.

Yvonne Morland, from A Book of Blessings

January 11

O God, who called all life into being,
THE EARTH, SEA AND SKY ARE YOURS.
Your presence is all around us,
EVERY ATOM IS FULL OF YOUR ENERGY.

Iona Abbey Worship Book

January 12

God, give me a moment to be still:
to listen for your voice in my heart.

Peter Millar, from Going Home Another Way

January 13

Let go the past;
loosen the thongs
that bind.

January

Love the present;
enjoy each shining
moment.

Look to the future
with courage
and hope.

Kate McIlhagga, from *The Green Heart of the Snowdrop*

January 14

Didn't you know?
Haven't you heard?
GOD OUR MAKER CARES FOR US
Didn't you know?
Haven't you heard?
JESUS OUR BROTHER WALKS WITH US
Didn't you know?
Haven't you heard?
THE HOLY SPIRIT LIVES IN US

Ruth Burgess, from *Bare Feet and Buttercups*

January 15

Our first task in approaching another people, another culture, another religion, is to take off our shoes, for the place we are approaching is holy.

Else we may find ourselves treading on people's dreams. More serious still, we may forget that God was here before our arrival.

Canon Max Warren, former General Secretary of the Church Missionary Society, in *For God's Sake Unity*

January 16

Cease seeing with the mind
and see with the vital spirit.

Chuang Tzu, in *Labyrinth*

January 17

Help me really live,
not just exist.

Martin Lönnebo, Carolina Welin, Carolina Johnasson, from *Pearls of Life*

January 18
Week of Prayer for Christian Unity

The word 'ecumenical' seems to make people's minds fly to the notion of churches bent on unity. That is a valid but secondary use of the word. The Greek *oikoumene* stands for 'the whole inhabited earth'. Fourteen uses in the New Testament are simply translated 'world'. Ecumenical commitment focuses not on the church but on the world God so loved that he sent his Son. The church then comes in as an agent of that love. Church unity must be shaped so as to forward God's will for the unity of the world in justice, truth and peace. Otherwise it may be self-serving.

Ian M. Fraser, from *The Way Ahead*

January 19

God of new beginnings,
help us to let go
and to turn our backs
on the things that hold us back,
and to hold on
to those things
that remind us of your love,
and help us to follow in your way.
Amen

From *Around a Thin Place*

January 20

Martin Luther King Day

Consider for a moment the statement of the Jewish mystic and theologian Abraham Joshua Heschel, who said of his experience marching with Dr Martin Luther King, Jr in Alabama, 'My feet were praying.' The meaning in our heads can become the meaning in our bodies. When we use our bodies with spiritual intent, both our bodies and the occasion become sacred. Sometimes these bodily actions accompany spoken prayers; sometimes they are prayers in and of themselves.

In saying 'My feet were praying,' Heschel meant that our bodies can *embody* prayer, or be places where prayer is actively happening ...

Jon M. Sweeney, from *Praying with Our Hands*

January 21

Abraham Joshua Heschel spoke of the ways in which God is no longer at home in the creation because we act as if God doesn't exist. Instead of being divine agents as we should, we effectively remove God from the world with our inaction. Heschel says: 'To pray means to bring God back into the world ... To pray means to expand God's presence.'

We pray with our bodies when we put them in front of tanks. We pray with our hands when we link arms together to fight injustice. We are co-creators with the Divine when we resist evil. The world is more sacred at these moments.

Jon M. Sweeney, from *Praying with Our Hands*

January 22

May your churches be centres of justice and joy, O Christ,
where your love is shared,
and your life made real in the world.

Brian Woodcock, from *This Is the Day*

January

January 23

We find it so difficult to dance in this life:

Carrying the burden of responsibilities
the pressures of every day
the memory of past partners
the weight of the world, it seems like, sometimes.

Afraid of what people might think
afraid of people judging us
(of God judging us)
afraid of looking foolish out there on the floor.

Afraid we won't get the rhythm right
afraid dancing is for the chosen few.
Feeling so weighed down with guilt and sin
we can't move with grace ...

O Christ, Lord of the Dance,
in you we live and move and
have our being.

Neil Paynter, from *Down to Earth*

January 24

Lord, help me to stop in my tracks today –
even for 10 seconds –
and discover again
where my true home is:

that place in your love,
where I always belong.

Peter Millar, from *Light of the World*

January 25

With people everywhere
WE AFFIRM
GOD'S GOODNESS AT THE HEART OF HUMANITY,
PLANTED MORE DEEPLY THAN ALL THAT IS WRONG.

Iona Abbey Worship Book

January 26

Lord Jesus, You are before us – directing.
We believe it.
That is what gives us courage to go on.
New challenges already beckon and again we sometimes dither.
But it is You that directs.
It is You that beckons.
So we dedicate ourselves.
And we bless You.

George MacLeod, from *The Whole Earth Shall Cry Glory*

January 27

Holocaust Memorial Day

Lord, remember not only the men and women of goodwill, but also those of ill will. Do not remember all the sufferings they have inflicted upon us; remember the fruits we bear, thanks to this suffering – our comradeship, our loyalty, our humanity, courage, generosity, the greatness of heart which has grown out of all this. And when they come to judgement, let all the fruits that we have borne be their forgiveness.

Prayer found on a scrap of paper beside the body of a girl who died at Ravensbrück, in *Growing Hope*

January 28

God bless each of us as we travel on.
In times of need
may we find a table spread in the wilderness
and companions on the road.

Jan Sutch Pickard, from *Blessed Be Our Table*

January 29

You love us, God.
You know us.
You know how we hurt ourselves
how we hurt each other
how we hurt your world.

We are sorry, God.
We want to change.
Help us and heal us.

Ruth Burgess and the children of Bellahouston Academy,
from *Praying for the Dawn*

January 30

If the only prayer you ever said was, 'Thank you,'
that would be enough.

Meister Eckhart, 14th-century Christian mystic, in *Growing Hope*

January 31

May beauty be before me. *(Stretch hands in front)*
May beauty be behind me. *(Stretch hands behind)*
May beauty be below me. *(Stretch hands down to feet)*
May beauty be above me. *(Raise hands toward sky)*
May beauty be all around me. *(Turn around, with outstretched arms)*

Traditional Navajo chant, from *Return Blessings*

January

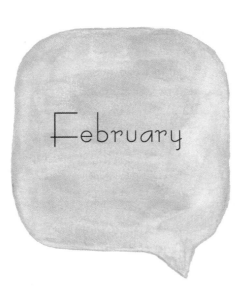

February 1

God of the journey, as we travel on
alert us to the things that matter
and open our eyes to every sign of your presence.
Give us a sense of direction,
or at least a sense of purpose,
a sense of wonder,
a sense that, in everything,
you are walking with us step by step,
gently leading us to the heart of things.

Brian Woodcock, from *Pathways for Pilgrims*

February 2

Candlemas

Light a candle, don't just curse the darkness.

A saying used by Iona Community member Stanley Hope, in *Growing Hope*

February 3

We are followers of one who loved the lost and the least, who identified himself with the outcast and the poor. The word of Jesus is that God runs out to the margins to meet us. The light shines from the margins, not the centre.

Kathy Galloway, from *Living by the Rule*

February 4

In the confidence of faith in our Creator:
WE CARRY THE LIGHT OUT INTO THE WORLD.
In the strength of the risen Christ Jesus:
WE CARRY THE LIGHT OUT INTO THE WORLD.
In the presence of the life-giving Spirit:
WE CARRY THE LIGHT OUT INTO THE WORLD.
Sharing the faith that the darkness will end:
WE CARRY THE LIGHT OUT INTO THE WORLD.

John Davies, from *Holy Ground*

February 5

Let me pause and be still for a moment
and remember that each day
the One who sustains all of life
offers me a place in which to rest my soul
so that I may grow in love.

Peter Millar, from *We Journey in Hope*

February 6

For those who have ears to hear and eyes to see, there are modern-day hints and signs, and parables of the Kingdom among the poor. (This should hardly surprise readers of the New Testament.) The Kingdom of God is somewhat elusive (now you see it, now you don't), but

February

there are glimpses, glimpses. These signs are not always 'religious'. They are often very, very earthy, to do with politics and neighbourliness and housing. There are many flowers in the concrete jungle.

Ron Ferguson, from *Bridging the Gap*

February 7

You are salt.
You have a tang of goodness
a saving grace –
and a taste of salvation.

Jan Sutch Pickard, from *Out of Iona*

February 8

Every day is a messenger from God.

Russian proverb, in *Growing Hope*

February 9

Jesus calls us
to leave the past
JESUS CALLS US TO HOPE

Ruth Burgess, from *Eggs and Ashes*

February 10

Jesus calls us
to travel lightly
JESUS CALLS US TO FAITH

Ruth Burgess, from *Eggs and Ashes*

February 11

Jesus calls us
to risky living
JESUS CALLS US TO LIFE

Ruth Burgess, from *Eggs and Ashes*

February 12

Jesus calls us
to live fairly
JESUS CALLS US TO JUSTICE

Ruth Burgess, from *Eggs and Ashes*

February 13

Through the process of self-examination, through repentance, through acceptance of our vulnerability and God's generosity, we may attain inner peace. But the message of the Gospel is quite clear: there can be

February

no inner peace without outer justice. We cannot rest content in the face of the world's need for healing and the sense of our complicity in the woundedness of the world (Isaiah 58:6-9).

Norman Shanks, from *Lent and Easter Readings from Iona*

February 14

Valentine's Day

O God, our lover.
We cling ourselves to you as a bride marries a groom.
You have called us into covenant with you,
no matter who and what we are.
We acknowledge your unconditional love that is freely given to us
through Jesus the Christ.
In this love, we are able to extend our hands to others.
May we continue to nourish this spirit of togetherness
that brings us into constant relationship with you. Amen

Kim S. Vidal, from *Moon Under Her Feet*

February 15

May God hold you as a lover,
may she caress your broken places,
may she dust you with gentleness,
and may you live in the world
as a sign of her touch.

Rosie Miles, from *A Book of Blessings*

February 16

Christ of the wilderness and of the crowded street,
whispering in the desert and shouting in the market,
help us to hear you above temptation's promises;
strengthen us to follow you on the highways of your world.

Helen Boothroyd and Richard Moriarty, from *Lent and Easter Readings from Iona*

February 17

God,
I thank You for the movement of coming out and coming in.
These holy energies sustain my life and foster evolution.
I let go of all that holds me back and blocks me.
I surrender myself into Your hands.

Urs Mattmann, from *Coming In: Gays and Lesbians Reclaiming the Spiritual Journey*

February 18

'In a world of electronic beeps and tunes it is silence after all
that feeds the soul.
Turn off the machines,
embrace the chattering mind that follows in their wake
and walk along gently into a stillness,
a space for peace.'

From *Labyrinth*

February

February 19

A few months ago, I took part in an Ignation retreat in Daily Life. The Ignation Sister who counselled me during that time posed many challenges to my preconceived ideas and one that has really stuck with me was the question of whether, given the necessary magic wand, I would choose to change James.

My initial glib reaction was 'Yes, I would wave my wand and make him heterosexual.'

But then I became aware of the danger in that kind of thinking. I could see that it was a little akin to wandering around the Tate Gallery or the Louvre with a paintbrush adjusting the various masterpieces with a few haphazard blobs of paint. Given the chance to 'fix' my son's sexuality, what havoc might I wreak with the whole person, with his refreshingly divergent mind, his creative talents, his zany sense of humour, his remarkable ability to empathise with the feelings of others?

Jacqueline Ley, from *No Ordinary Child: A Christian Mother's Acceptance of Her Gay Son*

February 20

World Day of Social Justice

God, lead us, that we may stand firm in faith for justice.
Teach us love. Teach us compassion.
Above all, out of love and compassion,
teach us to act.
Amen

Yousouf Gooljary, from *The Pattern of Our Days*

February 21

Our homeland is on earth
Our homeland is in heaven
WE ARE PEOPLE OF GOD

Our lives are commonplace
Our lives are full of wonder
WE ARE PEOPLE OF GOD

Ruth Burgess, from *Eggs and Ashes*

February 22

Because God is transcendent, always greater than anything we can think or imagine, we must never look on our faith as a package of truths which requires no further investigation. 'Faith,' as St Anselm wrote, 'seeks understanding', and there is no end to its exploration. True fundamentalism means letting God be the foundation of our minds and hearts, and God is mystery. Therefore the true fundamentalist will always be searching, always growing in understanding, will always welcome questioning, will be a careful and respectful listener to Christians of other denominations, to people of other religions and no religion. 'The fundamentalist' now connotes someone who enjoys absolute certainty about their version of Christian faith, who sees no need to explore other beliefs, because such exploration is a sign of weakness, and who is convinced that all their opponents are wrong and lacking in faith. The fundamentalist, in today's sense of the word, fails to bear witness to the holiness of God!

Gerard Hughes, from *For God's Sake Unity*

February

February 23

You know us, God.
We do not have to pretend with you.

Ruth Burgess, from *The Pattern of Our Days*

February 24

O Christ our enlightener,
once and for all,
you broke the link between suffering and punishment,
erased the line between deserving and undeserving
and invited the unseeing to open their eyes
to the truth about themselves.
Doing this, you revealed yourself,
became vulnerable.
Preserve us from the defendedness that makes us vicious,
give us insight to see the structures of injustice by which we profit,
and grace to cherish all people in our vulnerability,
knowing that we all live within your love.

Kathy Galloway, from *Lent and Easter Readings from Iona/Church Action on Poverty*

February 25

Bless to us, O God,
the earth beneath our feet.
Bless to us, O God,

the path whereon we go.
Bless to us, O God,
the people whom we meet.

Iona Abbey Worship Book

February 26

God dances in light
God delights in creation
GOD LOVES THE WORLD

God made the world
and all that is in it
GOD LOVES THE WORLD

Ruth Burgess, from *Eggs and Ashes*

February 27

What would the world look like if we were to open our fists and let go of our desire to be completely secure? What would our world look like if we opened our minds to the uncommon thought that creation has within it the *'essential goodness of God'* and we reached out an open hand to grasp another person's hand to form community? Our world would change drastically if we did as the Psalmist writes: *'I will abandon myself into your hands as long as I live.'*

Lisa Bodenheim, from *Disturbing Complacency*

February

February 28

Help us to accept, O Christ
that our paths may not be smooth
and our journeys may often be risky.

Help us to accept
vulnerability with no promise of security.
Help us to give you
devotion with no promise of reward.

John Davies, from *Lent and Easter Readings from Iona*

February 29

We may walk with him who is
the way, the truth and the life,
and find our freedom in your service
through Jesus Christ
Amen

Prayer from Durham Cathedral (adapted), from *St Cuthbert's Way*

March 1

World Book Day

O storyteller,
you sit me down
and fill me with tears
and love
and laughter.
Come into my life,
and tell your story
through me.

Ruth Burgess, from *Bare Feet and Buttercups*

March 2

With words:
we scribble and scrawl
we wrestle and pray
we wound and shame
we touch and heal
we praise and prophesy

May our words be grounded in your Word, O God.

Yvonne Morland, from *50 New Prayers from the Iona Community*

March 3

... God is in the business of seeking outcasts. Mercifully, his agenda is quite different from that element of the church that bears his name but continues to ostracise and demonise gay people. As long as this tragic state of affairs exists, I believe God will create individuals to be part of a group whose hunger for the knowledge of his all-embracing love is often cruelly denied.

So I thank God for all faithful gay Christians of whom God says, 'They are my servants ... in whom I will be glorified (Isaiah 49:3, NRSV). They alone are equipped for the Christlike ministry of entering into the special experience of a minority group.

Jacqueline Ley, from *No Ordinary Child: A Christian Mother's Acceptance of Her Gay Son*

March 4

Holy God
GIVE ME A HAPPY HEART
Wise God
GIVE ME A SEEKING MIND
Strong God
GIVE ME GENTLE HANDS
Pilgrim God
GIVE ME COURAGE AND JOY

Ruth Burgess, from *Eggs and Ashes*

March

March 5

Christians are explorers, not map makers.

George MacLeod, from *Daily Readings with George MacLeod*

March 6

Alexander Scott, the nineteenth-century Celtic teacher, uses the analogy of a plant suffering from blight. If such a plant were shown to botanists, even if the botanists had never seen that type of plant before, they would define it in terms of its essential life features. They would identify the plant with reference to its healthy properties of height and colour and scent. They would not define it in terms of its blight. Rather they would say that the blight is foreign to the plant, that it is attacking the essence of the plant. Now this may seem a very obvious botanical point. But maybe it is so obvious that we have missed the point when it comes to defining human nature. We have tended to define ourselves and one another in terms of the blight, in terms of sin or evil, in terms of the failings or illnesses of our lives, instead of seeing what is deeper still, the beauty of the image of God at the core of our being.

Philip Newell, from *Christ of the Celts*

March 7

Become pregnant with hope and longing.

Nicola Slee, from *Doing December Differently*

March 8

International Women's Day

Belonging to this global movement for change has been one of the great joys and privileges of my life. I have been inspired and moved by the courage, the wisdom, the humour, the persistence, the creativity – and not least by the righteous anger – of women in Palestine and Sri Lanka, in Romania and Zimbabwe, in Ruchill and West Pilton. We have heard the rhetoric, we have won some concessions, and yes, there has been truly significant social and cultural change in the status and opportunities available to at least some women in some places. But we've got a long way to go in this country, never mind in some of the poorest places on the planet. Gender equality and empowerment of women – that strikes me as the rallying cry for a radical transformation of the current global order. It calls for a major redistribution of resources, not just from the materially wealthy to the poor, but away from structures, traditions, symbols and systems which embed male power and privilege, limiting women's space and capacity for action.

Lesley Orr, from *Living Letters of the Word*

March 9

Scatter your visions into our dreams,
whisper your love song
on every breeze
until hearing, we turn,
and looking, we see,

and for every human, plant a tree,
for every newborn, clean a stream,
for every death,
set a caged bird free.

Annie Heppenstall, from *The Healer's Tree*

March 10

O God, star kindler
kindle a flame of love within us
to light our path in days of darkness.

Kate McIlhagga, from *The Green Heart of the Snowdrop*

March 11

O God, moonburnisher
burnish the shield of faith
that we may seek justice
and follow the ways of peace.

Kate McIlhagga, from *The Green Heart of the Snowdrop*

March 12

O God, sun warmer
warm us with your love
to melt the frozen hand of guilt.

Kate McIlhagga, from *The Green Heart of the Snowdrop*

March 13

Come to inhabit our darkness
Lord Christ,
for dark and light
are alike to you.

Kate McIlhagga, from *The Green Heart of the Snowdrop*

March 14

Jesus,
lover of life,
hear my crying
for those who die today
and for the pain that is in me and in the world.
Amen

David McNeish, from *We Journey in Hope*

March 15

'What do you know about politics?' we are asked. Or about the subtle workings of the economy? What do you understand about the complexities of political power, the sensitivities of the market, the difficulties of globalisation, of the intricacies of the law? Why don't you leave all that to the experts? And yes, mostly the church did leave all that to the experts – and look at the mess we are all in now!

Allan Boesak, from *The Fire Within*

March

March 16

The church might not be what the world calls 'expert', but it knows about justice. It might not be expert, but it knows what the Lord requires: to do justice, to love mercy, and to walk humbly with God. It might not be expert, but it knows the God who lifts up the poor from the dust of the earth, who breaks the bow of the mighty and the powerful, who teaches us that not by might shall one prevail. It may not be expert, but it knows that to do justice and righteousness, to judge the cause of the poor and the needy, is to know the Lord. It might not be expert, but it knows: without the love of God, the world shall perish. It might not be expert, but it understands that without the compassionate politics of Jesus, our politics is no more than calculated, secular casuistry.

Allan Boesak, from *The Fire Within*

March 17

St Patrick's Day

If you are going on pilgrimage to find Christ, you will only find him if you carry him in your heart.

Irish monastic saying, in *Growing Hope*

March 18

God, the promise of life in unfurling poppy petals,
spreading butterfly wings,
bursting buds,
and tiny, trusting hands

Joy Mead, from *Holy Ground*

March 19

St Joseph's Day

May we, like Joseph, be prepared to stand by quietly,
allowing others to be the centre of attention,
enabling others to fulfil their calling,
working in the background,
obedient to God and to none other.

Ian Cowie, from *Prayers and Ideas for Healing Services*

March 20

Green-hearted winter snowdrop,
symbol of God's renewing love,
turn your face to the sun,
as the days lengthen
and he sets his face to go to Jerusalem.

Kate McIlhagga, from *The Green Heart of the Snowdrop*

March 21

First day of spring

I love trees: they stand naked in winter, and burst with new life in spring. If you take a stethoscope on a spring walk and look for a young smooth-barked tree, you can hear what sounds like a heartbeat through the stethoscope: the sound of sap being 'pumped' against gravity, up the tree to the tips of the leaves. It sounds like our own heartbeat, and I often think of it as the heartbeat of creation.

Chris Polhill, from *A Heart for Creation*

March

March 22

World Water Day

When we turn the tap, clear, clean, fresh water pours out.
Most of the world's population are not so fortunate.
Let us commit ourselves to press the case for justice through:

OUR FAITH IN GOD THE CREATOR,
JESUS, THE LIVING WATER,
AND THE HOLY SPIRIT, FOUNT OF LOVE.

Katrina Crosby, from *Holy Ground*

March 23

God of rainbows,
confront the cynical.
Blow away the blasé.
Fill us with delight,
that we may celebrate the WOW!
in every person, every place.

Zam Walker, from *Iona: Images and Reflections*

March 24

The day Oscar Romero was assassinated

We commit ourselves to work for change
and put ourselves on the line;

to bear responsibility, take risks,
live powerfully and face humiliation;
to stand with those on the edge;
to choose life
and be used by the Spirit
for God's new community of hope.

Iona Abbey Worship Book

March 25

*International Day of Remembrance of the Victims of Slavery and
the Transatlantic Slave Trade*

For the pioneers who first led the struggle against slavery
For the courage of countless slaves who resisted the system
For the faith of those who saw the total inconsistency between
Christianity and slavery
and spoke out boldly
For all who today risk their lives to seek the truth
and expose the reality of modern slavery
For all who work and volunteer for organisations
concerned about those in bondage
God be praised.

Iain Whyte, from *Holy Ground*

March 26

Birthing, life-giving God
you have nourished us with your life-giving breast
and you taught us how to struggle against the dragons of our time.
Bless us as we gather to bring new visions for the world.
Fill us with your creative wisdom as we give birth
to a new heaven and a new earth.
Amen

Kim S. Vidal, from *Moon Under Her Feet*

March 27

I find myself bombarded with annunciations that become part of me
(incarnation), with the primary wonder of sunlight and tree bark, daisies
and seeds, a baby's hands and an old woman's face ... all part of a soaring
vision that begins with paying attention to everyday life – and exists
because of the greatest mystery, risk and hope of all – *that we can love ...
and go on loving.*

God of all love and every truth,
help us to look with open eyes ...

Joy Mead, from *Where Are the Altars?*

March 28

God of all hopefulness:
If we have made gold our hope,
forgive us.
If we have made success our confidence,
forgive us.
If we have rejected the cause of the poor,
forgive us.
If we have rejoiced in the ruin of others,
forgive us.
For in you alone is our hope.

Kate McIlhagga, *The Green Heart of the Snowdrop*

March 29

It is in the awe-filled silence before the glory of God that we find the courage to speak boldly in and to the world. Our souls tremble before God so that our knees won't have to tremble before kings. We are awed by the presence of the Living One so that we need not be overawed in the presence of earthly power. It is in the rest in God's mercy that we feed the restlessness within ourselves for the sake of justice.

Allan Boesak, from *The Tenderness of Conscience*

March

March 30

As I breathe so I pray
Amen

Rosie Morton, from *Friends and Enemies*

March 31

Dear God,
as we think of Jesus
we think not just of prayer and quiet retreat
but of a life of action,
of tables overturned,
of lives touched and healed,
endless walks through arid deserts
to the next place of hurt and need.

Prayer from the Resident group on Iona, from *Holy Ground*

April 1

April Fool's Day

Laughter

O shout of laughter
outburst of indecorous noise,
explosion of absurdity,
shaking the helpless body with glee,
puncturing the proud and the pompous;
you are the destroyer of convention:
come, upend our table of pomposity and pride
with your sudden detonations.

Richard Skinner, from *Invocations*

April 2

Christ, in this age of globalisation, we hear you calling us
to turn upside down the present unjust world order
so that your kingdom may come.
WE WILL ANSWER YOUR CALL.
WE CHOOSE TO SERVE YOU.
WE COMMIT OURSELVES TO PUT GOD BEFORE WEALTH
AND TO TAKE ACTION FOR JUSTICE IN YOUR NAME.
AMEN

Helen Boothroyd, from *Holy Ground*

April 3

We are rarely presented with positive and joyful images of Islam, yet this has been overwhelmingly my experience. One such experience was on a Friday evening at the beginning of a week of celebrations for the anniversary of the birthday of the Prophet Muhammad. My friend Assan took me to a large mosque in Bradford. The atmosphere was electric: many of the men were dressed in colourful traditional clothing, the smell of perfumes filled the air and I was greeted by many a passing stranger noticing my clerical collar and taking me warmly by my hand or greeting me with an open welcoming smile. When we finally managed to get into the main part of the mosque, after some simple food was served to us in the basement, I saw colourful banners adorning every side; ecstatic renditions of poetry to the Prophet were being recited and enthusiastically received by a congregation who exhibited a real sense of excitement, love and joy ...

Ray Gaston, from *A Heart Broken Open*

April 4

In You all things consist and hang together:
The very atom is light energy,
the grass is vibrant,
the rocks pulsate.

All is in flux; turn but a stone and an angel moves ...

George MacLeod, from *The Whole Earth Shall Cry Glory*

April

April 5

What kinds of betrayals are taking place in our modern world? Are we colluding?

Peter Millar, from *Iona Dawn*

April 6

Christ who forgave your killers,
teach me to pray for those who seem set against me.
Give me your peace, that my heart may be untroubled.
Give me your peace that I may not be afraid.

Annie Heppenstall, from *Reclaiming the Sealskin*

April 7

World Health Day

Economic systems in their turn influence the way that human beings develop. Mental health professionals know that altruism is a product of psychological health, while self-obsession is a sign of dysfunction. People who grow up in secure environments, feeling themselves and their vulnerability valued, are likely to mature as socially constructive, peaceable and happy to promote others' interests. Similarly, people who experience violence, fear and abandonment as children hand on all of these in their relationships.

Margaret Legum, from *It Doesn't Have to Be Like This*

April 8

Spirit of the living God, present with us now,
enter us
body, mind and spirit
and heal us of all that harms us,
in the name of Jesus.
Amen

Iona Abbey Worship Book

April 9

God help us to live fully and openly and hopefully,
to trust in grace
and believe in resurrection.

Neil Paynter, from *Friends and Enemies*

April 10

Loved into being,
hill, fen and field;
loved into being,
ocean flood and fish;
loved into being,
each plant and each tree;
loved into being,
you and me.

Kate McIlhagga, from *The Green Heart of the Snowdrop*

April

April 11

What is God like?
GOD IS CARING AND TENDER
What is God like?
GOD IS SLOW TO ANGER
What is God like?
GOD IS RICH IN KINDNESS
Maker, Jesus and Holy Spirit
GOD WELCOMES US WITH LOVE

Ruth Burgess, from *Fire and Bread*

April 12

As buds uncurl
and flowers open their faces to the sun,
turn us
to the light and warmth
of your presence.

Kate McIlhagga, from *The Green Heart of the Snowdrop*

April 13

Go out:
love wastefully and save the world.

Go out:
live foolishly and be wise.

Go out:
you cannot love too much.

Amen

Sally Foster-Fulton, from the download 'Love Wastefully and Save the World: A Liturgy for Monday of Holy Week'

April 14

Lord God, whose Son was content to die to bring new life, have mercy on your Church which will do anything you ask, anything at all, except die and be reborn.

Ian M. Fraser, from *The Way Ahead*

April 15

Whoever we are
WE ARE KNOWN TO GOD
Whatever we've done
WE BELONG TO GOD
Wherever we go
WE ARE LOVED BY GOD
Every day, every moment
GOD IS OUR FRIEND

Ruth Burgess, from *Fire and Bread*

April

April 16

We don't need a special place or time;
we don't have to travel to Emmaus:
any road and any table
we can meet you, Lord, again;
we can stay with one another any place,
any time.

Brian Woodcock, from *Iona Abbey Music Book*

April 17

O Christ, the Master Carpenter,
who, at the last, through wood and nails,
purchased our whole salvation.
Wield well your tools
in the workshop of your world,
so that we,
who come rough-hewn to your bench,
may here be fashioned
to a truer beauty of your hand.

Iona Abbey Worship Book

April 18

Come with us God,
come into the desert
the painful and lonely places

of our memories
of our lives.
Come with your angels
and bring us peace.

Ruth Burgess, from *Praying for the Dawn*

April 19

Creator God,
from quark to planet your universe is awesome.
Give us eyes to gape at the wonders daily about us,
and the will to live in the harmony of your creating.

Chris Polhill, from *Eggs and Ashes*

April 20

What if it was not Jesus's crucifixion that saves us? What if it was the way he lived his life that saves us? He told parables. He hung out with the socially unacceptable and the impure, healed people, and taught that the Community of God is at hand. Is it possible that Jesus would want us to focus on his lifestyle because that is what gives meaning to his crucifixion? It is not his crucifixion that saves us from our sins. It is his lifestyle, which led to his crucifixion, that saves us ... Through his lifestyle, Jesus showed us that God forgives us, that God's Community is near. For that, his disciples deserted him, the religious leaders condemned him to death and the Roman authorities killed him.

Lisa Bodenheim, from *Disturbing Complacency*

April

April 21

To become aware of the sacramental nature of the cosmos,
to be open to the sacramental possibilities of each moment,
to see the face of Christ in every person –
these things are not novel,
but their rediscovery is the beginning of our health.

Ron Ferguson, from *Chasing the Wild Goose*

April 22

Earth Day

The Iona Community has since its inception been committed to justice for and the wellbeing of people living in poverty. Increasingly people concerned with human justice and those concerned with eco-justice have seen how greatly these two are interconnected and interdependent ... when one part of the body suffers, all the other parts suffer with it, including the earth's body.

Kathy Galloway, from *Cherish the Earth*

April 23

There is no religious or moral rule to equal the demands of love. What people will remember of us is not what rules we kept, what creeds we believed, what doctrines we followed, but when we were kind, when we opened our hearts and minds to the sorrows, joys and fears of others and revealed something of our own weaknesses; when we rejoiced with the joyful and walked alongside the sorrowing, when we encouraged the fearful and protected the timid, when we gasped with wonder at a sunset, or expressed joy at the beauty of a flower, when we were hospitable, generous and forgiving, when we were open to the gifts of those seeking our own giftedness, when we made people feel included and valued ... both personally and politically. In other words, how we responded and connected.

Joy Mead, from *A Way of Knowing*

April 24

Stay with us Lord,
since the day is far spent and night is coming;
kindle our hearts on the way,
that we may recognise you in the scriptures,
in the breaking of the bread,
and in each other.
Amen

Iona Abbey Worship Book

April 25

The Jubilee called for a redistribution of land every fiftieth year to eliminate the inequalities of ownership. What different places some countries, where a privileged few people control much of the land, could be with such an ethic.

Ghillean Prance, from *The Earth Under Threat*

April

April 26

The real art is in discerning
when God is right under your nose:
familiar yet surprising,
comforting yet unexpected.

Judith Jessop, from *Fire and Bread*

April 27

What we really need is devotion to Jesus. Then, even if the theology and much else leave a lot to be desired, the Lord will work through us. He gave thanks that it was through 'spiritual babes' that wonders had been worked, while the clever clerics and the qualified Pharisees guddled around in their intellectual mazes.

Ian Cowie, from *Jesus' Healing Works and Ours*

April 28

Lord,
I ask only this:
that you would meet me
on the road;
and that I, expectant,
would recognise and know you
in your coming
and so find my life
transformed.

Pat Bennett, from *Around a Thin Place*

April 29

Personally consumed of the here and now,
we must recover the sense of God as
Here and Now.

George MacLeod, from Daily Readings with George MacLeod

April 30

From time to time, a particular Bible verse or passage moves me to tears, and Mark 14:51–52 (AV) did that for me recently. Judas has just betrayed Jesus ... His other disciples have deserted him and fled but we are told: 'There followed him a certain young man, having a linen cloth cast about his naked body. And the young men laid hold on him; and he left the linen cloth, and fled from them naked.'

There was something about the description of this young man that caught me on the raw, with its poignant picture of nakedness and vulnerability, coupled with the urgent, desperate desire to be with Jesus ...

As I read over those verses, the unknown young man seemed to personify painfully for me the plight of so many homosexuals, hounded away from Christ by the bigoted thuggery of some Christians, and I could hardly bear to keep reading.

Jacqueline Ley, from No Ordinary Child: A Christian Mother's Acceptance of Her Gay Son

April

May 1

International Workers' Day

May the earthly, everyday things
such as stables and mangers, offices and garages
be filled with a new glory
because of Jesus, who was born in a manger and worked at a bench,
Jesus who now works through his children.

Ian Cowie, from *Prayers and Ideas for Healing Services*

May 2

God is my lollipop lady:
I am safe with her.
She sees me across the busy junction
to find a safe place to relax.
She restores my faith in humanity
as she helps me to choose
the right time and place to cross.

Janet Lees, from *Word of Mouth*

May 3

World Press Freedom Day

God of the dispossessed,
show me how I can be in touch
with people like Cheikh Kone (of the Ivory Coast)

who is now without a home
because he spoke the truth.

Peter Millar, from *Our Hearts Still Sing*

May 4

God of familiar landmarks,
thank you for helpful signposts on the way.

Tom Gordon, from *A Blessing to Follow*

May 5

In joy and sorrow,
in gain and loss,
in despair and hope,
in death and life,
the Constant One,
calls me still.

Janet Lees, from *Tell Me the Stories of Jesus*

May 6

Wash me clean, God.
Forget the sprinkling with gentle showers
Tip a bucket of your forgiveness over me
Tumble me in the waves of your mercy
Drench me in the sea of your love.

Ruth Burgess, from *Praying for the Dawn*

May 7

For food that nourishes and
prayer that refreshes
in this fast and busy world –
thanks, God.

Neil Paynter, from *Blessed Be Our Table*

May 8

We affirm that we are made in God's image,
befriended by Christ,
empowered by the spirit.

Iona Abbey Worship Book

May 9

Today and tomorrow
Rooted in Jesus
WE GO INTO THE WORLD
TO BEAR MUCH FRUIT

Ruth Burgess, from *Fire and Bread*

May 10

There is a very old legend, and all legends that persist speak truth, concerning the return of the Lord Jesus Christ to heaven after His Ascension.

It is said that the angel Gabriel met Him at the gates of the city.

'Lord, this is a great salvation that Thou hast wrought,' said the angel.

But the Lord Jesus only said, 'Yes.'

'What plans hast Thou made for carrying on the work? How are all men to know what Thou hast done?' asked Gabriel.

'I left Peter and James and John and Martha and Mary to tell their friends, and their friends to tell their friends, till all the world should know.'

'But, Lord Jesus,' said Gabriel, 'suppose Peter is too busy with his nets, or Martha with her housework, or the friends they tell are too occupied, and forget to tell their friends – what then?'

The Lord Jesus did not answer at once; then He said in His quiet, wonderful voice: 'I have not made any other plans. I am counting on them.'

George MacLeod, from *Daily Readings with George MacLeod*

May 11

As the dry stane walls
enfold the fields,
enfold us, O God.

Kate McIlhagga, from *The Green Heart of the Snowdrop*

May

May 12

Great Spirit,
you are the answer to all of this world's yearning.
So will you come in power,
and will you come in peace,
and will you take up your living somewhere deep inside of me?

Glendon Macaulay, from *Dirt, Mess and Danger*

May 13

God of life,
forgive us for dealing in death
as we turn our back on our neighbours
and once again sink into the apathy
of dried-up religion.
As we take our next breath
may it be a holy inspiration
which fires us up to come out of our tombs
and live the life of your kin and kingdom.

Janet Lees, from *Word of Mouth*

May 14

World Migratory Bird Day

Go gently, my friends:
feel the good earth
beneath your feet,

celebrate the rising of the sun,
listen to the birds at dawn,
walk gently under
the silent stars,
knowing you are on holy ground
held in love –
in the wonder of God's creation.

Peter Millar, from *50 New Prayers from the Iona Community*

May 15

Conscientious Objectors' Day

Stand, O stand firm
Stand, O stand firm
Stand, O stand firm
and see what the Lord can do.

Song from the Cameroons, from *Many and Great*

May 16

May you see light and good in everyone
May you remain open to wonder and mystery
May you stand firm in the assault of the powers
(shielded with the armour of God
and a good sense of humour)
May you stay rooted in hope.

Neil Paynter, from *Holy Ground*

May

May 17

God help me to maintain a spirituality that is both tough and tender, and to seek you not only in the sacred places but in the midst and the margins of daily life.

Brian Woodcock, from *Gathered and Scattered*

May 18

Come, Holy Spirit,
make us a sign of God
in the darkness and poverty
in our world,
where hope is frail
and daily life
a struggle to survive.

Yvonne Morland, from *Holy Ground*

May 19

Love of God
GROW IN US
Fire of God
REFINE US
Laughter of God
DANCE IN US
Justice of God
DEFINE US
Tears of God

WEEP IN US
Beauty of God
CARESS US
Story of God
RUN DEEP IN US
Mystery of God
BLESS US

Ruth Burgess, from *Fire and Bread*

May 20

Every breath
you in me
me in you

Martin Lönnebo, Carolina Welin, Carolina Johnasson, from *Pearls of Life*

May 21

World Day for Cultural Diversity, Dialogue and Development

Dr Salah suddenly asked me one day, 'Do you believe in God?' I replied, 'Yes, I could never have done what I have been able to do if I had not had a firm faith in God, and it is my faith that keeps me going even though things do look bleak.' He said that he, too, had only been able to survive throughout the years of the civil war in Lebanon and to participate in the struggles of his people because he believed in God. He is a Muslim, I am a Christian, we both have our different beliefs and ways of worshipping God, but we both believe in a God of Justice and Mercy.

Runa MacKay, from *Exile in Israel*

May

May 22

International Day for Biodiversity

I will eat this cherry as if it were the first and last from the tree
I will savour this peach as if it were the only one
I will relish this mango as if it were the harvest of paradise
I will worship this fruit as if it were the body of God.

Nicola Slee, from *Blessed Be Our Table*

May 23

Perhaps the task, our need in communion with God and in reflective prayer, is to sit in the observation car at the rear of the train. There, we can see where we have come from, see this and that fall into its proper place, find a perspective, and believe and know that if our God has guided us thus far, we can trust him enough to take us on to the next stage.

Tom Gordon, from *A Need for Living*

May 24

Rehab Daher, who used to work with me, is the best student in her class in the Hariri Nursing School in Sidon. It was Rehab who said to me one day, 'You know, Doctora, I cannot hate anyone.' Her father was killed in the fighting when she was very small. Her smiling face always makes me think of the words of Jesus in St Matthew's Gospel: 'The eye is the lamp of the body. If your eyes are good, your whole body will be full of light.'

Runa MacKay, from *Exile in Israel*

May 25
UN Africa Day

Eat and drink together,
talk and laugh together,
enjoy life together,
but never call it friendship
until you have wept together.

An African saying, in *Growing Hope*

May 26

Sent by the Lord am I;
my hands are ready now
to make the earth the place
in which the kingdom comes.

The angels cannot change
a world of hurt and pain
into a world of love,
of justice and of peace.
The task is mine to do,
to set it really free.
Oh, help me to obey;
help me to do your will.

Nicaraguan Song, from the oral tradition,
translation by Jorge Maldonado, from *Sent by the Lord*

May

May 27

A few years ago on Iona, I met a woman in her seventies who shared with me the story of her spiritual journey. She had grown up in the southern United States. It was her family's custom to attend church every Sunday. One particular Sunday morning nearly sixty years ago, she was sitting in church when, halfway through the liturgy, a dog wandered into the sanctuary. It sauntered up the central aisle, sensing its way forward, until it got to the altar.

There it stopped and began to sniff around. No, it did not do what you think I am going to say! It turned around and left. It did not like what it smelled. 'That is when I left the church,' the woman said to me. 'It didn't smell right. It didn't smell natural.'

It was a dog that guided this woman to see as a young adolescent that her religious environment did not smell right, that it had lost the connection between the natural and the holy, between spirit and matter, between God and creation. Her experience is eccentric in its details but it is the story of countless numbers of women and men in the Western world today.

Philip Newell, from *Christ of the Celts*

May 28

Help me to let go
Help me to trust you God
help me to trust my friends
help me to put down the hurt of my living
help me to let go.

Ruth Burgess, from *Friends and Enemies*

May 29

The trouble with the Church today is that nobody wants to persecute it. Nobody wants to persecute it because there is nothing really to persecute it about, don't you think?

George MacLeod, from *Growing Hope*

May 30

Christ has no other hands but your hands
to do his work today;
no other lips but your lips
to proclaim the good news;
no other love but your love
to give to the rejected, the lonely,
the persecuted, the marginalised.

Based on a prayer by St Teresa of Ávila, in *Holy Ground*

May 31

Jesus has entered into every experience and feeling known to humankind. He alone is qualified to deal with homosexual Christians on how to live their lives.

Jacqueline Ley, from *No Ordinary Child: A Christian Mother's Acceptance of Her Gay Son*

May

June 1

When Merton asked Thich Nhat Hanh what he had learned in his first year in the monastery, Nhat Hanh replied: 'How to open and close doors quietly.' This struck Merton – and it still strikes me today – as a profound insight into our spiritual lives. This young Buddhist monk was not consumed with studying great texts or memorising chants and liturgies (although, of course, he had done that too). He wasn't focusing on becoming a spiritual master. He was practising his faith with his thought (mind), will (heart) and actions (body) – with his life, and he was doing it in little, ordinary ways.

Thich Nhat Hanh's Buddhist tradition teaches that it is important to cultivate mindfulness in everyday life – becoming aware at every moment of the spiritual meaning in things and in our actions.

Jon M. Sweeney, from *Praying with Our Hands*

June 2

God, we give you thanks
for your Holy Spirit
plummeting into our lives
like a gannet –
white wings
cleaving the grey waves –
disturbing, delighting
and defying death. Amen

Jan Sutch Pickard, from *50 Great Prayers from the Iona Community*

June 3

The Spirit of the Lord is upon me:
HE HAS CHOSEN ME TO BRING GOOD NEWS TO THE POOR.
HE HAS SENT ME TO PROCLAIM LIBERTY TO THE CAPTIVES
AND RECOVERY OF SIGHT TO THE BLIND;
TO FREE THE OPPRESSED
AND ANNOUNCE THAT THE TIME HAS COME
WHEN THE LORD WILL SAVE HIS PEOPLE

Affirmation based on Luke 4:18-19, from *Praying for the Dawn*

June 4

May God keep us in all our days,
may Christ shield us in all our ways,
may the Spirit bring us healing and peace.
May God the Holy Trinity
drive all darkness from us
and pour upon us blessing and light.

Kate McIlhagga, from *The Green Heart of the Snowdrop*

June

June 5

World Environment Day

I thank
the whisper
of oak,
the rowan blood,
the field
the folk
the violets
which grow
in the litter
and mould.

Alison Swinfen, from *Through Wood*

June 6

Everything I do is related to the whole.

Kay Lindahl, from *The Sacred Art of Listening*

June 7

In September 1940, when the incendiary bombs were raining on London, it looked as if the rebuilding might have to be stopped because of lack of timber. Then the deck cargo of a Swedish ship carrying wood from Canada had to be jettisoned. The timber floated all the way to Mull, directly opposite Iona – all the right length.

'Whenever I pray,' said the beleaguered Dr MacLeod, 'I find that the coincidences multiply.'

From *George MacLeod: A Biography*, by Ron Ferguson

June 8
World Oceans Day

Dear God,
you made the beautiful butterfly
and the funny frog.
You made the gentle breeze
and the roaring ocean.
Help us look after all these beautiful things.

Nancy Cocks, from *Growing up with God*

June 9
St Columba's Day

Christ, draw near to us, little people, trembling and most wretched, rowing through the infinite storm of this age, and bring us safely to the most beautiful haven of life.
Amen

Attributed to St Columba, in *Good News of Great Joy*

June

June 10

O God,
help us to admit our fragility
and to be gentle with each other.

Neil Paynter, from *Growing Hope*

June 11

Our hearts are set on pilgrim roads not to satisfy ourselves with finding one holy place, not to romanticise this thin place, but to take the experience of the presence of the Holy back into the thick of things ...

Murphy Davis, Open Door Community, Atlanta, Georgia, from *Around a Thin Place: An Iona Pilgrimage Guide*

June 12

Refugee Week

Well-travelled, wandering God of compassion,
as you have led your people to a land filled with milk and honey,
so we invoke your guidance to the millions of refugees
all over the world ...
We remember them in our prayers that they may seek refuge in lands
where they would be welcomed.
Fill us with your Spirit
that we may open our hearts to the strangers in our midst.
Fill us with compassion to love the unloved neighbour.
Make us your instruments for a community where love abounds.
Amen

Kim S. Vidal, from *Moon Under Her Feet*

June 13

You are an island in the sea, O God,
you are a hill on the shore,
you are a star in the darkness,
you are a staff to the weak.
O, my soul's healer,
when I am lost and tired and stumbling
you shield and support me.
God, help me to give light, love and support to others.

Adapted from the *Carmina Gadelica*, in *Living Letters of the Word*

June 14

A spirituality of politics means walking humbly with God. It is not closeted, albeit pious, immobility. It is a *walk*, a way of life guided by strategy, but sustained by faith, made possible by policy, but nurtured by prayer. It is a private and public acknowledgement of our utter dependence upon God, of our openness to be called upon by the authority of the poor. We are engaged in politics, not simply to 'help' others, but because we are compelled by justice; not because we believe the poor need help, but because we believe they deserve justice. For us justice is not a philosophical concept or a legal definition or an ideologically adapted and approved slogan. It is, as the prophet Micah has taught us, the act of humbly walking with God.

Allan Boesak, from *The Tenderness of Conscience*

June

June 15

When you were busy, surrounded by crowds,
with their needs and their pleading,
you always had time for one more individual,
just because at the heart of your kingdom,
there was infinite compassion.

John Polhill, from *A Heart for Creation*

June 16

Loving God, Creator,
you are far more generous than we know how to be.
Like a father
greeting his prodigal son who had wasted the family inheritance:
you run to meet us;
you lavish yet more upon us;
you welcome us back home.

Brian Woodcock, from *Iona Dawn*

June 17

Lord of the excluded,
open my ears to those I would prefer not to hear;
open my life to those I would prefer not to know;
open my heart to those I would prefer not to love;
and so open my eyes to see
where I exclude You.

Pat Bennett, from *Around a Thin Place*

June 18

God of my weariness,
give me what I need to keep on going.

Tom Gordon, from *A Blessing to Follow*

June 19

'For me it's the birds feeding, the leaves falling, the wind blowing, the branches nodding at me, anybody who comes and surprises me by his or her wonder and thoughtfulness. Becoming a deep, real, honest, compassionate human being who, using poetry, art, music, curiosity, is truly alive to everything – that's the journey and that's where most of us make our most profound discoveries. I think God is to be found in the depths of our humanity and not in any particular religious exercise.'

Donald Eadie, from *Words and Wonderings*

June 20

World Refugee Day

O Jesus, you belonged to a refugee family. We pray for the millions of displaced people in our world, and for the opening of borders to the nationless.

Iona Abbey Worship Book

June

June 21

In the late Middle Ages, the poets and singers of Scotland were known as 'Makars', makers. It is not too fanciful to imagine the universe as the song of God the Makar, a joyous outpouring of energy and creativity and wild ordering and continuous exchange. And it is truly a religious instinct to respond to God's song-making with our antiphon of praise. Creation makes worshippers of us.

Almighty God, Creator:
the morning is Yours, rising into fullness.
The summer is Yours, dipping into autumn.
Eternity is Yours, dipping into time.
The vibrant grasses, the scent of flowers, the lichen on the rocks,
the tang of seaweed,
all are Yours.
Gladly we live in this garden of Your creating. (George MacLeod)

Kathy Galloway, from *Cherish the Earth*

June 22

May God who is Alpha and Omega
be present in all our world's endings, endurings and beginnings,
to bless, sustain and renew all creation
and to work the redemption and completion of all time.

Nicola Slee, from *A Book of Blessings*

June 23

Economics is about how people relate to each other around resources and work. Essentially it is about the needs of people in relation to those things. If the system doesn't serve people, we can change it. Economics is not about the logic of a system: it is about people and how they are being served by whatever system we are using. The point needs making not because it is easy to design economic systems that meet the needs of people, but because discussion of economics in recent years has been bedevilled by the carefully fostered idea that what is happening now is inevitable.

Margaret Legum, from *It Doesn't Have to Be Like This*

June 24

song in the silence
irrepressible laughter
long peace

let go
let go
let go
always let go

always receive

Kathy Galloway, from *The Dream of Learning Our True Name*

June 25

It has become fashionable to say: 'I have no faith.' People no longer trust their own senses: their ears, eyes, nose, and they don't trust their hands. René Descartes questioned the existence of the world and then said: 'I think, therefore I am.' For goodness sake, it's all about more than the mind. You can hear, see, smell, taste, touch ... you can love.

Satish Kumar, from *Words and Wonderings*

June 26

International Day in Support of Victims of Torture

God give us peace,
but not at the expense
of those who are hungry
or whose labour is exploited;
not so dictators kill and torture
or armies bully and destroy;
not so some are excluded
for others to be comfortable.
Give us peace with Your justice.

Chris Polhill, from *A Pilgrim's Guide to Iona Abbey*

June 27

The 'spiritual' people, who consider any active involvement in peace and justice issues to be a contamination of true religion, have not read the Bible

... the activists, who commit themselves to issues of peace and justice, but ignore prayer, are in danger of acting aggressively and unjustly towards their opponents or sinking into cynicism and despair. The Bolshevik revolution began with the highest ideals and ended in mass persecution, murder and destruction.

Gerard Hughes, from *For God's Sake Unity*

June 28

Grant us, Lord, that balance
of action and stillness,
of work and play
that fits the wholeness you intend for us.
Help us to see that all is prayer;
all things part of life with You.

Chris Polhill, from *A Pilgrim's Guide to Iona Abbey*

June 29

Solemnity of Saints Peter and Paul

'Sometimes I feel overwhelmed. There is so much to do! ... But then I remember what St Paul said in Corinthians: We all have gifts. Some folk are good on the barricades, some are good at writing letters ... We can't do everything: We are all pieces of the jigsaw ... We are all sparks of Light ...'

An Iona Community member, at a plenary meeting,
from *Light of the World*

June

June 30

World Friendship Day

God bless you,
friends and strangers who held me;
through trouble,
through fear,
through trembling weakness.

Chris Polhill, from *A Pilgrim's Guide to Iona Abbey*

July 1
Gay Pride Day

May the One
who has lovingly created human life with such diversity and potential,
be with all who challenge prejudice and abuse of power
and all who work for a fairer, more inclusive society.

Brian Woodcock, from *This Is the Day*

July 2

We're one in Christ our Master,
a holy, hallowed race
in whom all rainbow people
are due a welcome-space,
all sorts and shapes and sizes
caught in God's wide embrace.

Ian M. Fraser, from *A Storehouse of Kingdom Things*

July 3

Christ,
Wherever two people love each other honestly,
You are present in that love.
We thank You for every couple that understands their relationship
as a gift from You.

Urs Mattman, from *Coming In: Gays and Lesbians Reclaiming the Spiritual Journey*

July 4

Lord Jesus, You are beneath us.
We believe it.
When we slip, You catch us.
When we kick You in the face, You just serve us.
And when we pack in and fall right down,
You come further down just to be beside us.
In awe we thank You.

George MacLeod, from *The Whole Earth Shall Cry Glory*

July 5

May you always notice
the dazzling, beautiful white flowers
growing up between the cracks.
And may your road be
full of little resurrections.

Neil Paynter, from *A Book of Blessings*

July 6

And the great Spirit who loves us
and has given us our true names
whispers them in darkness
when we are alone
when we are weary
when we are despairing

and we are re-membered
in the heart of God.

Kathy Galloway, from *The Dream of Learning Our True Name*

July 7

Neither eight hundred years ago, nor yesterday
are these flesh and bones redeemed;
but now in this moment
as we put our trust in Thee
we are made new.
New creatures we become.
The inner flesh of our immortal bodies – vibrant to eternity.

George MacLeod, from *The Whole Earth Shall Cry Glory*

July 8

We believe in a bright and amazing God,
who has been to the depths of despair on our behalf;
who has risen in splendour and majesty;
who decorates the universe
with sparkling water, clear white light,
twinkling stars and sharp colours ...

Iona Abbey Worship Book

July 9

Deep peace of the running wave to you,
deep peace of the flowing air to you,
deep peace of the quiet earth to you,
deep peace of the shining stars to you,
deep peace of the Son of peace to you.

Iona Abbey Worship Book

July 10

When I believe
there are no miracles left
(at least, for me)
tickle me
with your grace
till I ache
with life.

Thom M Shuman, from *Bare Feet and Buttercups*

July 11th
Feast of St Benedict

To Benedict, listening is not the same as intellectual comprehension. Listening, as Benedict understood it, is a special kind of deep attentiveness to all of life. Benedict understood that we can live in ways that either dull or sharpen this attentiveness. Benedict's Rule is a guide to sharpening the ears of the heart.

Daniel Homan, o.s.b and Lonni Collins Pratt,
from *Radical Hospitality*

July

July 12

We also need to recover a sense of the strength of God's protective and enfolding love. Celtic prayers of protection speak powerfully to many who find themselves lost or hurt in today's brutal and stressful world. During a period as part-time chaplain at a psychiatric hospital, I myself found them particularly meaningful for those suffering from depressive illness and schizophrenia. The use of prayers in the *lorica* (breastplate) or *caim* (encircling) traditions may, indeed, have distinct therapeutic value in the treatment of psychiatric illness. Some people who have experienced drug or alcohol addiction or sexual abuse are gripped by a sense of demonic possession and the almost physical reality of dark and malevolent forces. In this respect they can relate to the world of Columba and perhaps they can be helped by the kind of prayers that he used to create circles of protection.

Ian Bradley, from *Columba: Pilgrim and Penitent*

July 13

As the grey wave
creeps on to the shore
and the sail limps
for port,
so, Lord, do I
seek harbour,
crawl into the circle
of your welcoming arms.

Kate McIlhagga, from *The Green Heart of the Snowdrop*

July 14

God of the morning.
Wake us up.
Wake us up to wonder.
Wake us up to beauty.
Wake us up to justice.
Wake us up to love.
God of the morning.
Wake us up.
Wake us up good.

Ruth Burgess, from *Bare Feet and Buttercups*

July 15

This is Your day Lord
and I thank You for its freshness and possibility.
Help me to go through this day
not worrying too much about how it will work out,
but knowing that You hold me, and all of the world,
in Your hands.
And when evening comes
may my heart know
Your calm and Your light.

Peter Millar, from *Pathways for Pilgrims*

July

July 16

God of the journey's twists and turns,
help me to trust your strength when I am scared.

Tom Gordon, from *A Blessing to Follow*

July 17

In a free-market economy, the criteria for evaluation are extrinsic, they are set by the market. Value is added. Anything – a house, a painting, a car – is worth only what it commands in the market. The shift to having this as the criteria for relationship is well underway. Our society is inclined to measure the worth of people by how useful, productive, beautiful, successful they are, and to undervalue those who are not these things. Christian community should, we believe, be genuinely counter-cultural, because it affirms diversity, and the intrinsic value of all its members, regardless of their utility, rarity or success.

Kathy Galloway, from *Bread for the Road*

July 18

Small stuff
The hair on your head,
the yeast in the flour,
the mustard seed in the palm of your hand;
all this counts with Jesus
and remember
you count too.

Janet Lees, from *Tell Me the Stories of Jesus*

July 19

'On the other side,'
said the man from Nazareth.
'Throw your nets on the other side.'
And curiously
they did
and their lives
changed.

David Osborne, from *Iona: Images and Reflections*

July 20

Today
may I give and receive love.
Today and every day.

Ruth Burgess, from *Bare Feet and Buttercups*

July 21

All I can say is that if God 'cares more' about confessional consensus than about the possibility that all children eat enough and laugh, I do not want that unity.

If God 'cares more' about proper rites of baptism and ordination than about our ability to love one another across boundaries of faith /unfaith/class/religion/colour/sex/education/status, this is not a God I want to worship, nor one I believe in.

July

As human beings, we live in a cosmos faced with death.

Unity, 'for God's sake', is about the strange hope that there is life stronger than death – that 'quite different things are going on'. That is unprovable. But maybe worth believing.

Elizabeth Templeton, from *For God's Sake Unity*

July 22

'That's right, it's not retreat. [Iona is] a peaceful place but not a passive place. It's an active place where you can be renewed, invigorated, inspired to communicate with the world, to go back, whether to Glasgow or London or wherever you come from, to work for transformation, for justice and peace, for equity in the world ... all that George MacLeod stood for. I feel personally that when I went to Iona I was re-energised to be on the front line.'

Satish Kumar, from *Words and Wonderings*

July 23

May prayer feed your actions
and may your actions feed the world.

Neil Paynter, from *Holy Ground*

July 24

Christ in us meets the needs of those who come, not us,
for we have nothing to give them —
only Christ in us.

Ian Cowie, from *Prayers and Ideas for Healing Services*

July 25

[There is a] famous scenario where a man waits in a crowed café for his
friend, and the friend does not come. And Sartre writes, 'My friend who
was not there was more present than all the people around me in the
place.'

Elizabeth Templeton, from *For God's Sake Unity*

July 26

It's a long time since we saw anyone walk on water.
Today's heroes can't do it;
celebrity lifestyle splashed across the tabloids;
documentary exposés, and world exclusives
sold for more than silver.
If it happened today, would the media just report
'Jesus of Nazareth cannot swim'?

Janet Lees, from *Tell Me the Stories of Jesus*

July

July 27

Prayer, as I see it, has no power to manipulate or coerce but is about mindfulness, being with, being alongside in unknowing, those who suffer … or rejoice, something like reaching out to others and making their sickness, hunger, anguish, nakedness our own. And that's much harder than muttering a few intercessions. The incredible risks of love have to be something more than pretty prayers.

Joy Mead, from *Words and Wonderings*

July 28

Come to us Creator God
so that we may praise you.
Wrest the clutching shadow from us
cast it into cloth for stars.

Yvonne Morland, from *A Book of Blessings*

July 29

Dear Jesus,
be with me when I feel sad and when I feel mad.
When I do something wrong, help me say,
'I'm sorry.'
When someone says 'Sorry' to me,
help us forgive each other and be friends again.
Amen

Nancy Cocks, from *Growing up with God*

July 30

International Day of Friendship

Forgiving God, we believe that you called us
to be salt and light;
that you offer us time and space and strength
to begin again.

Iona Abbey Worship Book

July 31

God is like a silent guest at a party, easily ignored, but if we give the silent
one attention, he or she may turn out to be the most interesting person
there.

Gerard Hughes, from *For God's Sake Unity*

August 1

Lammas Day/Harvest

You are the bread of life: You are the whole loaf.
And we are the particles: we the flour: You the leaven.
A great mystery is Your Church.

George MacLeod, from *The Whole Earth Shall Cry Glory*

August 2

O Treasure,
dandelion in the concrete,
gold in the field:
Come call us to search for You
in the waste places of the world.

Ruth Burgess, from *Hear My Cry*

August 3

It is easy to assume that all we need to know about God, Jesus, the Holy
Spirit and our faith lies between the covers of the Bible. Did God only speak
to us in the past – in particular, the past recorded in the Bible? Does God
no longer speak to us in the present or in the future? What happens when
we allow the Bible, sacred though it is, to be God's only voice? If the Bible
does not point us toward God, but instead speaks for God, then the Bible
has become our god.

Lisa Bodenheim, from *Disturbing Complacency*

August 4

Job was called to let God be God. Even with all our scientific insight, what we know about the universe is so much less than what is still mysterious to us. The created order in all its complexity and beauty moved a quantum physicist to say that the appropriate response to it is one of sheer wonder and love. But such a celebration requires the dethronement of human ego, and the birth of co-operation with nature rather than domination over it.

Kathy Galloway, from *Cherish the Earth*

August 5

Thank you
for the people you sent
when I needed them most –
for the insight,
the touch,
the smile,
that showed what God was like.

Tom Gordon, from *A Need for Living*

August 6

The Feast of the Transfiguration

Either we walk on the poor and we'll end with Hiroshima, or we walk with the poor which will end in Transfiguration.

Source unknown, in *Growing Hope*

August

August 7

The spring of machair and the sucking squelch of bog
High cairns
Low, wet patches of cottongrass
Falling asleep between two hills like in the hollow of God's hand
and being woken up by cows.
A path.

No path.

Neil Paynter, from *Iona: Images and Reflections*

August 8

'You want a place where you can be serene,
that will let you contemplate and connect
two consecutive thoughts,
or that if need be,
can stir you up,
as you were made to be stirred up,
until you blend with the wind
and water and earth
you almost forgot you came from.'

From *Labyrinth*

August 9

Nagasaki Day

'Doubtless you members of the jury would agree that sabotaging the ovens of Auschwitz would have been a moral duty. The movable incinerator that is Trident is many times more lethal.'

Ellen Moxley, Trident Ploughshares 2000 defendant, in *Growing Hope*

August 10

How unlike the North American woodland Indians we are. They often think in terms of the consequence of their actions upon the seventh unborn generation. Contemporary life is geared to the length of political office.

Ghillean Prance, from *Earth Under Threat*

August 11

People
places
institutions
situations
can put me down.
God
only
ever
wants
to raise me up

August

and love me.
Alleluia
Amen

Ruth Burgess, from *Friends and Enemies*

August 12

International Youth Day

We pray for all young people who struggle in our cities: to find their place, hold their own, even to just feel OK. May they catch a glimpse of something better – a topsy-turvy kingdom where the last come first. May they have hope.

Ruth Clements McQuaid, from *Iona: God's Energy*

August 13

God, our Creator,
we come together
to celebrate your creation:
the bright beauty about us,
the abundance of your providing;
accept this offering of praise
as we worship you,
the Maker of all.
Amen

Chris Polhill, from *A Heart for Creation*

August 14

We pray for people in places of suffering,
whose names only you and their friends
and families know,
and whose lives you cherish ...
God in your mercy
hear our prayer.

Ruth Burgess, from The Pattern of Our Days

August 15

We wander the streets,
yearning to find you,
calling your name,
but it is only
a single mother who turns
and wearily smiles,
a street person
who whispers 'hello',
a little girl who pirouettes
and takes our hand.
But you are still here, Lord.
Help us to see.

Thom Shuman, from Fire and Bread

August

August 16

The blessing of Martha's welcome,
the blessing of Mary's listening;
the blessing of action,
the blessing of reflection
the blessing of a God
who is in each of these,
and in each one of us,
be with us all.
Amen

Iona Abbey Worship Book

August 17

For the promises I have made
then broken,
forgive me, Lord.
Of my outward show
and inward poverty,
heal me, Lord.
In my desire to produce fruit
and in my struggle,
help me, Lord.

Kate McIlhagga, from *The Green Heart of the Snowdrop*

August 18

Is that You,
whispering one,
urging me secretly to walk
in the garden's singing time
with You?

Anne Heppenstall, from *The Healer's Tree*

August 19

The more closely I examine the foundation of the Christian faith in the biblical texts, the more I am convinced that the problem is not a lack of an environmental ethic, but rather an under-emphasis on certain parts of the Judeo-Christian teaching ...

'The Lord God took the man and put him in the garden of Eden to till it and keep it.' Two interesting commands were given to the first people: to till and to keep the land. The Hebrew word *abad*, translated 'till', also means 'to serve', and the English 'keep' in Hebrew is *shamar*, to watch or preserve. This is quite different from the frequent misinterpretation of what dominion means. We are actually told to serve and preserve the land!

Ghillean Prance, from *Earth Under Threat*

August

August 20

Dance, calls the waves
but I will not dance.
Sing, calls the wind
but I will not sing.
Weep, sighs my soul
and I weep
and I dance
and I sing.

Jim Hughes, from *Growing Hope*

August 21

Help me to be a doer and not just a hearer or a speaker.

Ralph Morton, in *Growing Hope*

August 22

We ask You to make us expectant,
instead of planners:
We ask You to make us seekers,
rather than know-alls.
We ask You for grace
so that we are ready to receive.

George MacLeod, from *The Whole Earth Shall Cry Glory*

August 23

You can't kill the spirit, she's like a mountain.
Old and strong, she lives on and on and on.

Traditional, from Return Blessings

August 24

As the poor widow welcomed Elijah,
let me be open
to the richness and miracle in meeting.
As Abraham and Sarah welcomed passing strangers,
let me entertain the possibility of
angels in disguise.
Let my eyes be opened
that I may recognise in my neighbour
the divine presence of Christ.

Iona Abbey Worship Book

August 25

By your healing of the diseased
Lord, heal the sick

By your fortitude in the storm
Lord, calm the fearful

By your fondness for little children

August

Lord, protect the young

By your labour at a bench
Lord, hallow our work

By your forgiveness on the cross
Lord, pardon our sins
By your rising from the dead
Lord, give us life.

From an evening liturgy, Gorbals Group Ministry, 1957–1974,
from *Bridging the Gap*

August 26

A number of years ago, I delivered a talk in Ottawa, Canada ... I referred especially to the prologue of the Gospel of John and his words concerning 'the true light that enlightens everyone coming into the world' (John 1:9). I was inviting us to watch for that Light within ourselves, in the whole of our being, and to expect to glimpse that Light at the heart of one another and deep within the wisdom of other traditions. At the end of the talk, a Mohawk elder, who had been invited to comment on the common ground between Celtic spirituality and the native spirituality of his people, stood with tears in his eyes. He said, 'As I have listened to these themes, I have been wondering where I would be today, I have been wondering where my people would be today, and I have been wondering where we would be as a Western world today if the mission that came to us from Europe centuries ago had come expecting to find Light in us.'

Philip Newell, from *Christ of the Celts*

August 27

God the Maker,
thank you for making me
just as I am.

Chris Polhill, from *A Pilgrim's Guide to Iona Abbey*

August 28

Hope has two beautiful daughters. Their names are Anger and Courage:
Anger at the way things are, and Courage to see that they do not remain
the way they are.

Attributed to St Augustine of Hippo, in *Growing Hope*

August 29

International Day Against Nuclear Tests

Loving God, we remember and pray in solidarity with those who work for
peace in the face of the threat of war and fear of nuclear destruction.

We pray for all who have been victims of nuclear testing, dumping or
bombing. Help us to remember the sufferings of those who are still deeply
wounded in body and spirit.

We pray for lands and seas which have been contaminated and for the life
which depended on them.

We pray for politicians and policy-makers, that they may be

guided in the ways of peace.

Lord hear us ... Lord graciously hear us.

Kathy Galloway, from *Holy Ground*

August 30

We must look for God first in whatever it is that most perplexes us, whatever it is that lies closest in our field of view. For many, myself included, that will be in the mess of life: the stuff that went wrong, the prayer that wasn't answered, the event that knocked away the certainties of 'life before'. Indeed, we can put this thought more strongly: we must look for God in the very place where he is apparently absent. If we think we have found him anywhere else, then he will continue to be absent from that part of our lives that most needs to be healed, and that most needs an explanation.

Peter Longson, from *God in the Dark*

August 31

May you meet God
in every place, in every person
and in the depths of your own heart.

Jan Sutch Pickard, from *A Book of Blessings*

September 1

We are omnipotent,
able to order and destroy
according to our design.

Yet the turn of the leaf in morning sun
and the catch in our throat
drives us to our knees
and into prayer.

Yvonne Morland, from *Pushing the Boat Out*

September 2

'Be still and know that I am God!' The meaning of 'be still' in this verse is literally 'let go'. Let go, in the sure knowledge that God himself will act, like relaxing into free fall, in the confident certainty that the parachute will open at the crucial moment.

Jacqueline Ley, from *No Ordinary Child: A Christian Mother's Acceptance of Her Gay Son*

September 3

May our journey ahead
be blessed with
God's laughter,
silences,
risks,
challenges,
healings,

questions,
promises,
protests,
answers,
tears,
solidarity,
often uncomfortable peace and
compassion-filled surprises –
perhaps all in one day.

Peter Millar, from *Our Hearts Still Sing*

September 4

Let my wounds not hinder me
from venturing out always anew.
Show me the gifts
that lie in my woundedness and vulnerability.
Guide me to act with healing in this world.

Urs Mattmann, from *Coming In: Gays and Lesbians Reclaiming the Spiritual Journey*

September 5

Genuine spirituality is not cozy, and seldom makes you comfortable. It challenges, disturbs, unsettles, and leaves you feeling like someone is at the centre of your existence on a major remodeling mission. While affirming how wonderful you are, better than you really know, spirituality is also meant to change you. If it doesn't, it is something less than spirituality.

Daniel Homan, o.s.b and Lonni Collins Pratt, from *Radical Hospitality*

September

September 6

If we have become apathetic and complacent,
and over-relaxed and easy,
let us understand your presence
as the restless wind of adventure.

Glendon Macaulay, from *Dirt, Mess and Danger*

September 7

Do not retreat into your private world,
there are more ways than firesides to keep warm;
there is no shelter from the rage of life,
so meet its eye, and dance within the storm.

Kathy Galloway, from *Iona Abbey Music Book*

September 8

The sound of 'sheer silence' is God's gift to Elijah, who has been hasty, violent, fearful, competitive ... Seeking refuge in a cave, subjected to a sequence of natural forces, he suddenly discovers God is not in this blustering but in the underlying stillness. This is a discovery from God that cuts through our own blustering and our experience of frightening forces around us – they are not God. This Word asks us to be patient and let the storm pass, to sit a while in our safe space and listen, really listen. Elijah takes refuge in a cave; none who take refuge in God will be condemned (Psalm 34:22).

Annie Heppenstall, from the download 'Be Still and Know that I am God'

September 9

Go out into the world to meet people
and find them no longer strangers
but fellow travellers;
no longer aliens to be avoided
but family to be welcomed;
no longer enemies to be feared
but friends to be enjoyed.

Pat Bennett, from *Acorns and Archangels*

September 10

The arms race and the war industry is not divided East/West, not even
North/South ... It is in fact an assault on the poor.

Helen Steven, from *This Is the Day*

September 11

The power of love is greater than the love of power.

George MacLeod, in *Growing Hope*

September

September 12

The soaring birds, the wild beasts,
the farm animals, the friendly pets praise you.
The angels, the whole company of heaven,
your whole family on earth, praise you.
We join their praise – we praise you.

Ian Reid, from *Meditations from the Iona Community*

September 13

God, help me to live more simply
and with greater faith in you. Amen

Neil Paynter, from *Going Home Another Way*

September 14

'What a wonderful world it is,' George MacLeod said, 'provided you believe
in another world. Not over against this world, but interlaced with it.'

Lisa Bodenheim, in *Disturbing Complacency*

September 15

I came to know George MacLeod in his later years. I realise now that part
of his greatness was that he did not mind repeating himself. And he lived
until he was ninety-six so he had plenty of opportunity to repeat himself.
One of the things he loved to say was, 'Matter matters, because at the heart
of the material is the spiritual.' What we do to matter, therefore, is at the

heart of our spirituality, whether that be the matter of our bodies and how we touch one another in relationship individually and collectively, whether that be the matter of the earth's energies and how we handle and share its goodness, or whether that be the matter of the body politic and how we approach one another's sovereignty as nations. These are holy matters. And it was because MacLeod believed that the Presence is deep within matter and that Creation is the Body of God that he committed himself and inspired others to what he called 'non-violence of heart and action'. He tirelessly preached peace.

Philip Newell, from *Christ of the Celts*

September 16

Journeying with you, Creator God,
is to journey in your world,
full of marvels and such beauty.
To glimpse eternity in sky and sea,
to feel the earth and rock beneath my feet.

Chris Polhill, from *50 Great Prayers from the Iona Community*

September 17

Journeying with you, brother Jesus,
is to journey with your friends.
To meet and travel a while together,
then part at the crossroads,
knowing you are with us all.

Chris Polhill, from *50 Great Prayers from the Iona Community*

September

September 18

Journeying with you, Holy Spirit,
is to journey with the wind.
To move to your wild music
then try to sing your song
so others may hear.

Chris Polhill, from *50 Great Prayers from the Iona Community*

September 19

What I believe can be summed up in five words: God is love; people matter.

Stewart McGregor, from *Growing Hope*

September 20

The Buddha was once asked, 'What makes a person holy?' He replied, 'Every hour is divided into a certain number of seconds and every second into a certain number of fractions. Anyone who is able to be totally present in each fraction of a second is holy.' There is nothing common about common life – it takes an awakened sense to see what is mysterious in each ordinary moment, to ponder in our hearts, to really see people and things – not our preconceptions of them.

Joy Mead, from *A Way of Knowing*

September 21

International Day of Prayer for Peace

Who brings about peace is called the companion of God in the work of creation.

Jewish saying, in *Growing Hope*

September 22

Act as if Jesus ruled now. And as you pray for God to pour down His mercy on you, you had better take a pretty stout umbrella. Firstly, because if you really act in faith, a lot of people will throw things at you, and secondly, because you will feel such a spring shower of forgiveness coming down on you that it will soak you!

But at last you will feel carefree, you will feel justified by faith, not in a textbook sense but in an overwhelming sense.

George MacLeod, from *Daily Readings with George MacLeod*

September 23

In the intertwining of my life with yours
restlessness meets peace.

Pat Bennett, from *Around a Thin Place*

September

September 24

In the intertwining of my life with yours
selfishness meets servanthood.

Pat Bennett, from *Around a Thin Place*

September 25

In the intertwining of my life with yours
death meets resurrection.

Pat Bennett, from *Around a Thin Place*

September 26

May those without shelter
be under your guarding
this day, O Christ.
may the wandering find places of welcome ...

Philip Newell, from *Each Day & Each Night*

September 27

The frustrations of this day:
the people who have made us feel uncomfortable;
the places we never wanted to be;
the situations we would rather not have found ourselves in;

the relationships, or the lack of them,
that are giving us cause for concern.
In the stillness, tell God about the matters that occupy your mind ...

Glendon Macaulay, from *Dirt, Mess and Danger*

September 28

Walking together
Singing psalms
Breaking bread
Pouring wine
Arguing fiercely
Speaking truth lovingly
Dancing on the earth
Spinning with the stars ...

O God, we are your followers
going where you lead us.

Yvonne Morland, from *50 New Prayers from the Iona Community*

September 29

Give me all the bent and broken Christians.
The ones who know they're weak and full of strife.
Who walk in spite of rain and embrace the joy and pain
as they celebrate the wonder of this messy life.

David McNeish, from *Living Letters of the Word*

September

September 30

O Christ, you are within each of us.
It is not just the interior of these walls:
it is our own inner being you have renewed.
We are your temple not made with hands.
We are your body.
If every wall should crumble, and every church decay,
we are your habitation.

George MacLeod, from *Iona Abbey Worship Book*

October 1

International Day of Older Persons

There's more I need to show
if you can take the time with me.

The album of my life,
just waiting
to be opened up again.

Tom Gordon, from *Holy Ground*

October 2

International Day of Non-violence

It's not enough that we say no to violence ourselves, even though that can be a good place to start. As an individual I have to consider whether in my everyday life I contribute to violence or oppression, for example through the goods I buy or how I invest my money.

Annika Spalde, from *A Heart on Fire*

October 3

Walk well your journey
in peace and in justice.
May you be wrapped
in the shawl of God's loving.

May you be cherished.
May you be blessed.

Ruth Burgess, from *A Book of Blessings*

October 4

Feast of St Francis

Lord of St Francis, hound us still
That money lose its hold
Lest, in the end, not stigmata
Should mark our hands, but gold ...

Ian M. Fraser, from *Eggs and Ashes*

October 5

World Teachers' Day

Education is as much a cradling of the soul as it is a feeding of the mind.

Ewan Aitken, in *Growing Hope*

October 6

Bless my pathway Lord
lead me in your teaching

Yvonne Morland, from *A Book of Blessings*

October

October 7

The church on earth and in heaven is always a sacred mystery. When it loses the 'sense of mystery' at its heart it becomes less and less aware of the Spirit's many unexpected surprises.

Peter Millar, from *Iona Dawn*

October 8

Dear God, you are the source of everything we have.
Yours is the vision of abundance,
and the light of our vision:
Bless our longing for your Kingdom,
our hunger for shared bread, wine and joy;
and our striving for their incarnation.
Amen

Margaret Legum, from *Gathered and Scattered*

October 9

Lord Jesus,
it is so wonderful to know of the spirit which You sent
and which even now invades our hearts.
By whose invading even now we know
that our thinking, feeling and willing are made new.

George MacLeod, from *The Whole Earth Shall Cry Glory*

October 10

World Homelessness Day

O Jesus, you identified with the naked and with those
who had no place to lay their heads.
We pray for the thousands of homeless men and women,
old and young,
in our cities.

Iona Abbey Worship Book

October 11

Traveller king,
when we go into our fine buildings
to worship you with silver cups and silk garments,
exquisite choirs and sumptuously crafted stone and wood,
somehow I think I know where you are.
You are just outside lying on a bench in the sun
resting your thorn-torn head for a while,
until we will come out and spare you some change for a coffee.

Annie Heppenstall, from *Wild Goose Chase*

October 12

Prayer is really good fun, can become good fun, and the future of our
Church is going to be funny until we can write that sentence.

George MacLeod, from *George MacLeod: A Biography*

October

October 13

Stand in one place,
feel pace slowing.
Instead of racing –
being, growing.

Andrée Heaton, from *Doing December Differently*

October 14

When politics and policies are biased to the poor
THEN SHALL THE LIGHT SHINE FORTH LIKE THE DAWN
When none go hungry and good food is for all
THEN SHALL THE LIGHT SHINE FORTH LIKE THE DAWN
When all have a safe place to call home and feel welcome
THEN SHALL THE LIGHT SHINE FORTH LIKE THE DAWN

Rachel McCann, from *Growing Hope*

October 15

St Teresa of Ávila called the rosary 'a chain uniting heaven and earth'. Mystics in many traditions have regarded prayer beads as similarly important. As our hands make their way around the strand, we – and our prayers – are woven into the fabric of the Divine.

Jon M. Sweeney, from *Praying with Our Hands*

October 16

World Food Day

Food three times a day. Some food every third day.
We live in an unjust world.
As our bodies are nourished, nourish our anger at injustice, we pray.
Amen

Ian M. Fraser, from *Blessed Be Our Table*

October 17

International Day for the Eradication of Poverty

By your solidarity with the outcast and the rejected
you honoured their humanity
and released their potential.
Forgive us our arrogance
and our stupidity;
open our hands and our hearts
to receive the gifts they bring;
and show us how to work together
so that the curse of poverty
may be outlawed from the earth.

John Harvey, from *50 New Prayers from the Iona Community*

October

October 18

We believe in God's Son amongst us,
sowing the seed of life's renewal.
He lived with the poor
to show the meaning of love.

John Harvey, from *Fire and Bread*

October 19

A person can feel discouraged taking on institutional structures and systems alone. An individual does not feel able to make a huge impact on our international organisations. Yet, as Jesus says, *'The kingdom of heaven is like a mustard seed that someone took and sowed in his field; it is the smallest of all the seeds, but when it has grown it is the greatest of shrubs and becomes a tree, so that the birds of the air come and make nests in its branches.'* We can start taking notice and voicing our analyses of the structures of our world. What a wonderful sense of camaraderie and encouragement there is, when we meet with people who share the same concerns as we do. What joy to meet and share with the people whom we seek to support.

Lisa Bodenheim, from *Disturbing Complacency*

October 20

In the silence you spoke to me, God,
of wordless peace, of depth and calm.
God of the silence, I am silent with you.

Tom Gordon, from *A Need for Living*

October 21

In the moment you spoke to me, God,
that moment of mystery, of wonder and love.
God of the moment, I share this moment with you.

Tom Gordon, from *A Need for Living*

October 22

In the laughter you spoke to me, God,
of life and hope, of fun and purpose.
God of the laughter, I laugh with you.

Tom Gordon, from *A Need for Living*

October 23

In the comfort you spoke to me, God,
of touch and breath, of warmth and tender care.
God of the comfort, I know comfort with you.

Tom Gordon, from *A Need for Living*

October 24

Don't ask why 'God doesn't speak'.
Don't stand amazed at his apparent deafness.
Don't half listen for his voice somewhere beyond the storm.
IT IS THE STORM THAT IS HIS VOICE ...

George MacLeod, in *This Is the Day*

October

October 25

You wrestle with me
question me
take me seriously
I bless the honesty of your love.

Ruth Burgess, from *Friends and Enemies*

October 26

May we discover that the road we didn't choose,
didn't want to travel,
is a highway that leads unerringly
towards the light.

Francis Copsey, from *A Book of Blessings*

October 27

Could not this amazing diversity of creation and the variety of our seasons
be an expression of God's love? As Creator of our universe, God seems to
say, 'How do I love? Let me show the many and varied ways ...' God shows
infinite love through the slow unfurling of tree and flower buds in spring,
the verdant heaviness of storms in summer, the harvest colours and
pungent smells of autumn, and the pristine beauty of evergreen boughs
and naked brown trees draped with white snow in winter.

Lisa Bodenheim, from *Disturbing Complacency*

October 28

May God write a message upon your heart,
bless and direct you,
then send you out
living letters of the Word.
Amen

Neil Paynter, from *Iona Abbey Worship Book*

October 29

I believe in
the sound of water over rocks,
waves on the shore;
in the possibility of stones
turning into sand,
on the way to becoming
nothing.

Joy Mead, from *Where are the Altars?*

October 30

I'm far too small a saint
than I would want to be.
I've been too big a sinner
once again.

October

So use this little saint –
it's all that I can be –
in place of me the sinner.
Please! Amen

Tom Gordon, from *New Journeys Now Begin*

October 31

When my time comes
please, please, please
no penguin parades,
no solemn posturing:
but folk in jeans,
children playing, babies crying
and dancing in the streets.

Ian M. Fraser, from *Friends and Enemies*

November 1

All Saints' Day

'In the Eucharist there are testimonies to communion with each other, with the family around the world, with rich and poor, hungry and thirsty ... and also testimony to those who've gone before us, who have died: the communion of saints. My experience through the years, particularly at simple early morning communions, is that some widows or widowers come not necessarily because they want some Eucharistic ritual, but because it's a place of giving thanks for those who have died and gone home and who are with God. At one level they are gone, we know it, there's the rawness of grief; at another level there is a continuing sense of presence ... a mysterious communion ... but the Eucharist can also be a place where we are brought into this mystery of absence and presence. Jesus, or his spirit, isn't under a white cloth. All the white cloth is telling us is that at the heart of all life, dark and light, creative and destructive, there is the profound mystery of the presence of the creative spirit of God. It doesn't always feel like that. Often it feels like a silence, an absence ... an abyss ... but the paradox of absence and presence is built into being human.'

Donald Eadie, from *Words and Wonderings*

November 2

All Souls' Day

Every creature is Yours
most awesome One,
and in death the breath
of each returns to you.

Annie Heppenstall, from *The Healer's Tree*

November 3

World Community Day

Today I shall dream –
of people together,
loving, sharing, eating, dancing

Joy Mead, from *Making Peace in Practice and Poetry*

November 4

'We were aware that there were other Christian groups whom we thought
were "pie in the sky" and didn't care tuppence about other people; who
thought that the Church really existed to help them live their lives, and not
to help other people live their lives. We got fed up with what we regarded
as their smugness and their lack of concern about what was really wrong
with the world. The Gospel had to be proclaimed and lived out, outside the
safe place. Our business was to change the conditions for the people of
the world who couldn't. It was to bring God's Kingdom on earth.'

From *Outside the Safe Place: An Oral History of the Early Years
of the Iona Community*

November 5

Weep over injustice,
rejoice in goodness,
love outrageously.

Joy Mead, from *Where are the Altars?*

November

November 6

Give blessings,
share joy,
live in gratitude.

Kay Lindahl, from *The Sacred Art of Listening*

November 7

Help us to see pattern and purpose,
and our part
in the weaving of the world.
Amen

Jan Sutch Pickard, from *Out of Iona*

November 8

Lord of the earth and sky,
as Martha did
I welcome you into the house of my heart;
as Mary did
I welcome you into the home of my thoughts:
In service,
in listening,
I welcome you.

Kate McIlhagga, from *Dandelions and Thistles*

November 9

International Day Against Fascism and Anti-Semitism

First they came for the communists, and I didn't speak out
because I wasn't a communist.

Then they came for the trade unionists, and I didn't speak out
because I wasn't a trade unionist.

Then they came for the Jews, and I didn't speak out
because I wasn't a Jew.

Then they came for me and there was no one left to speak out for me.

Attributed to Pastor Martin Niemöller, in *Growing Hope*

November 10

Lord of Life, let me breathe deeply
of your Spirit,
that my life may become a living prayer,
my thoughts ever mindful of your empowering presence.

Annie Heppenstall, from *Reclaiming the Sealskin*

November

November 11

Remembrance Day/St Martin's Day

'I am Christ's soldier and I cannot fight.'
For the God of peace, you put your sword away;
and with heart aching for a poor man's plight,
gave him half your cloak one bitter winter's day.

Kathy Galloway, from *Candles and Conifers*

November 12

Creator of All Things Living ...
We confess that we ... have abused your creation
through ignorance, exploitation and greed.
We confess doing permanent damage to your handiwork.
We confess to alienating ourselves from the Source of All Life.
We confess that we have forgotten who we are ...
Forgiving Creator, awaken us to the roaring of creation,
the cries for ecojustice,
that we may open our minds and hearts to respond.

Diann L. Neu, from *Return Blessings*

November 13

'Sometimes I collect pebbles from the shore near where I live.
The beach has pebbles of many sizes,
with different colours, from different rocks.

They were jagged once,
with sharp edges, and rough sides.
But now, over time,
with the movement of the waves and the grinding of the sand,
they are smoothed down, rounded and soft to the touch.'

Tom Gordon, from the download 'A Framework for a Memorial Event'

November 14

Darkness

O darkness
as potent as a curse,
as fragile as a candle flame,
as threatening as a foe,
as comforting as a friend;
you are the womb for all qualities:
come, endow us with your fecundity,
enrich us with your every paradox.

Richard Skinner, from *Invocations*

November 15

And You are love: uncalculating love.
When we kick You in the teeth,
Your sole concern is whether we have stubbed our toes.

George MacLeod, from *Growing Hope*

November

November 16

International Day for Tolerance

At the monastery everyone is a guest, not just the visitor at the door, but the monks themselves. God is the host, but God also becomes the guest we receive in others. In the monastic image of the world, we are all guests, we are all travelers, we are all a little lost, and we are all looking for a place to rest a while.

Daniel Homan, o.s.b and Lonni Collins Pratt, from *Radical Hospitality*

November 17

Jesus, stiller of storms,
still the storms in our hearts and minds,
the rage of anger, the turbulence of fear,
and bring us your peace.

Kathy Galloway, from *Friends and Enemies*

November 18

Take us into silence, God of all.
Embrace us with the silence
out of which the universe was made.

Janet Lees, from *Word of Mouth*

November 19

I am your child, my God,
help me grow,
help me mature

Martin Lönnebo, Carolina Welin, Carolina Johnasson, from *Pearls of Life*

November 20

Universal Children's Day

Practising wonder is all about combating the emotional bluntness caused by our society of excess. As children we have a natural curiosity about the world. As adults we have to actively support this curiosity so that it doesn't fade away among our other plans and projects. So often we walk around lost in our own thoughts without noticing what is around us. Wonder is about perceiving reality as it is, because beauty exists everywhere.

Touch leaves, flowers and other natural things. Pick them up, examine them.

Be open to beauty in unexpected places: patterns in the pavement, an old person's face, a fly cleaning its wings.

Go with a child on a journey of exploration. Allow yourself to be filled with joy at the things you discover together. Don't be afraid of being childlike.

Annika Spalde, from *A Heart on Fire*

November

November 21

World Television Day

God,
help me to remember
and to act upon the fact that
people in the world go on suffering
long after they have disappeared
from my TV screen.

Neil Paynter, from *Going Home Another Way*

November 22

Every creature is a word of God. Monks, mystics and teachers throughout church history echo this truth. Every creature is an address from God: a word, a question to which we can reply with love.

Annika Spalde, from *Every Creature a Word of God*

November 23

Dear God,
I remember times when somebody called me a name that hurt me inside.
I remember times when I called somebody a name
because I was mad.
Help me use words to make people feel better.
Call me by my own name and remind me
that you love me in Jesus' name. Amen

Nancy Cocks, from *Growing up with God*

November 24

To enter the majestic Amazonian forest for the first time is an awe-inspiring experience. The tall trees, many with buttressed trunks, give the forest a cathedral-like appearance ... this is very different from a Middle Eastern garden of Eden, but to the naturalist, this is a paradise because of the great variety of plants and animals which the forest contains, and the fascinating way in which the different organisms react.

Ghillean Prance, from *The Earth Under Threat*

November 25

International Day for Elimination of Violence Against Women

Spirit of love, under your strong and tender wings there is refugee for all who are exploited, harassed, patronised, demeaned and abused. Shield, nurture and restore us to wholeness and integrity, in our personal and corporate lives. In your shelter, let us create a safe place to be ourselves, to explore new possibilities, to share friendship and to sustain each other in the struggle for liberation.

Lesley Orr, from *The Pattern of Our Days*

November 26

When the child within us
points to the old man selling poems
or stares with wet eyes at the weeping homeless woman
or sways to the solitary melody of a saxophone outdoors
let us forget our destination
for a moment.

Emily Walker, from *Gathered and Scattered*

November

November 27

I do not believe that the *gospel*, which means 'good news', is given to tell us that we have failed or been false. That is not news, and it is not good. We already know much of that about ourselves. We know we have been false, even to those whom we most love in our lives and would most want to be true to. We know we have failed people and whole nations throughout the world today, who are suffering or who are subjected to terrible injustices that we could do more to prevent. So the gospel is not given to tell us what we already know. Rather, the gospel is given to tell us what we do not know or what we have forgotten, and that is who we are, sons and daughters of the One from whom all things come. It is when we begin to remember who we are, and who all people truly are, that we will begin to remember also what we should be doing and how we should be relating to one another as individuals and as nations and as an entire earth community.

Philip Newell, from *Christ of the Celts*

November 28

We behave as though creation is a force that needs to be conquered and tamed. We create large, single-species factory farms with thousands of cows deep in mud, or pigs on concrete floors, or chickens kept in individual cages. We uproot windbreaks to create bigger fields. We plant large areas with a single species of corn, soybean or grain, generously applying chemicals to eliminate both benevolent and malevolent plants and insects. When we stress uniformity and the need to control, we endanger God's gift of abundance, diversity and structure.

Lisa Bodenheim, from *Disturbing Complacency*

November 29

International Day of Solidarity with the Palestinian People

The wall of separation (two haiku)

Behind it
real lives are invisible:
the blank face of denial.

Geology of oppression:
a scar
would take an earthquake to shift.

Jan Sutch Pickard, from *Between High and Low Water*

November 30

St Andrew's Day

Don't forget that, in the Parable of the Last Judgement, those whom Jesus affirms do not even recognise him and have no religious words in their response. They exercise straightforward secular responsibilities: feeding the hungry, giving drink to the thirsty, clothing the naked, giving hospitality to the stranger, caring for the sick, visiting prisoners. That is enough to merit his 'Well done!'

Ian M. Fraser, from *Living Letters of the Word*

November

December

December 1

World Aids Day

Lord, have mercy.
Christ, free us.

Help us to roll away stones,
lift heavy conditions,
heal divisions,
to share with our sisters and brothers
the bread of life –
food, water, medicine, love.
Amen

Neil Paynter, from *Holy Ground*

December 2

International Day for the Abolition of Slavery

We confess that our standard of living still rests on the slavery to debt endured by so many in our world. Poor people denied medical, educational and social facilities in order that their governments may repay interest to the rich world.

We confess that we shop or bank uncritically, enabling profits to be made from children enslaved on cocoa farms or in rug-making factories, and men and women imprisoned in labour camps.

We confess that all too often we close our ears to the cries of women exploited in sexual slavery or domestic servitude because we don't want to believe that this happens in our society.

God forgive, and lead us to open our ears and raise our voices.

Iain Whyte, from *Holy Ground*

December 3

A candle burns,
the sign of our hope.
God of hope,
come to us again this Advent.
May your hope live within us,
burning as a light in our lives.

David Hamflett, from *Candles and Conifers*

December 4

So frayed, so frazzled,
so harried, so hassled ...

We might not hear the voice calling to us:
'Prepare the way, the Lord is coming ...'
Open our ears, Lord, open our ears.

Thom Shuman, from *The Jesse Tree*

December

December 5

Lord, in these weeks of waiting for You
help us to be touched
by all the small signs of peace and joy
which are
in our midst.

Peter Millar, from *Light of the World*

December 6

O sun of Justice,
O Bright Morning Star,
herald of light and joy:
Come, shine in our darkness and bring us hope.

Ruth Burgess, from *Hear My Cry*

December 7

I have been stumbling around in dark alleys for too long, God.
I am not expecting you to show me an easy way out;
but I am crying out for you to come and find me,
to let me know you are with me
in the darkness.

Brian Woodcock, from *Advent Readings from Iona*

December 8

God, help us to hear your voice through the babble of this world
where words are used to confuse, distract, manipulate, sell illusion,
buy power;
help us to be still and receptive to your healing,
encouraging,
inspiring,
enduring,
life-giving
Word ...

Neil Paynter, from *Light of the World*

December 9

International Anti-Corruption Day

'Why have you failed?' a World Bank expert asked Julius Nyerere, the former President of Tanzania, at a Washington meeting. He replied, 'The British Empire left us a country with 85% illiterates, two engineers and 12 doctors. When I left office in 1985, we had 9% illiterates and thousands of engineers and doctors. At that point our income per capita was twice what it is today – after the Structural Adjustment programme. We now have one third less children in our schools, and public health and social services are in ruins. During those years, Tanzania has done everything that the World Bank and the IMF have demanded. So I ask you: 'Why have you failed?'

From *It Doesn't Have to Be Like This*, by Margaret Legum

December

December 10

World Human Rights Day

The [present] system automatically creates a steeply graded playing field in favour of the rich. In that process the values of human solidarity, human equality and intrinsic human rights find no place. The idea that there is something fine and humane in a society of equals is inevitably seen as sentimental and inefficient. Periodic acts of charity replace intrinsic justice as a means to ameliorate the fate of excluded people. The Christian promotion of Jesus's 'bias to the poor' finds no place in official policies.

Margaret Legum, from *It Doesn't Have to Be Like This*

December 11

O Disturber,
herald of life and change:
Come drag us from our safe havens
and plant our feet on the road of life.

Ruth Burgess, *Hear my Cry*

December 12

Love is our awareness of God's coming in someone else.

Ralph Morton, in *Growing Hope*

December 13

O God,
You love me:
Come,
come quickly.
I need Your help.

Ruth Burgess, from *Hear my Cry*

December 14

May our love be as wild as fire
as free as the wind
as deep as the earth
as gentle as a running stream.
May our love bring to birth a child.

Mary Taylor, from *Friends and Enemies*

December 15

O Emmanuel,
God among us, beside us, within us:
Come into our communities, our homes, our lives.
Come quickly, and stay.

Ruth Burgess, from *Hear my Cry*

December

December 16

Advent.
Once a year
the chance to wait
with a purpose.
Makes a change.

Carolyn Morris, from *Candles and Conifers*

December 17

It is only with the eyes of love that we'll see His coming.

Ralph Morton, from *Growing Hope*

December 18

Many of the great democratic social movements of the 20th century were about the people on the margins, the people written out of history, saying, 'We are here too. Stop overlooking us. We will no longer be invisible. Include us in.' So part of rebuilding the common life involves recognising that the historically dominant voice in both the church and the world, that of heterosexual, able-bodied, successful white men, is not the only voice, and about listening to the voices from the margins.

Kathy Galloway, from *Living by the Rule*

December 19

Bless to us, O God, the road that is before us.
Bless to us, O God, the friends who are around us.
Bless to us, O God, your love which is within us.
Bless to us, O God, your light which leads us home. Amen

Ruth Burgess, from *Candles and Conifers*

December 20

The box would be pretty big and awfully heavy, understanding God, but perhaps this year I will package up all my hurt, all my anger, all my grudges, and give them to you, that I might have enough room to receive your Child into my heart.

Thom Shuman, from *The Jesse Tree*

December 21

I love rhythm
spring, summer, autumn, winter
Lent, Easter, Advent, Christmas
Jack Frost, bluebells, full moon, conkers ...
Thanks for all the seasons, God.

Ruth, Burgess, from *Going Home Another Way*

December

December 22

Cynic in you, become a child again.

Nicola Slee, from Doing December Differently

December 23

In your quiet hidden way,
come to heal and save.
Incognito, in our streets,
beneath the concrete, between the cracks,
behind the curtains, within the dreams,
in ageing memories, in childhood wonder,
in secret ponds, in broken hearts,
in Bethlehem stable, still small voice,
Word of God, amongst us.

Brian Woodcock, from Advent Readings from Iona

December 24

Christmas Eve

Once again, we welcome you
bending so low to creep in among us,
not forcing, not shouting,
too gentle to even flicker our candle flames.
Make your home among us again, we pray;

be our guest, in heart and home and city,
in the empty, howling wastelands of our times,
and light up our world once again
with the new hope
and the new life
that faith in you still brings.

John Harvey, from *Going Home Another Way*

December 25

Christmas Day

A few years ago, I read an extraordinary little piece about Christmas in the newspaper. It described how Richard Lewis, the Bishop of St Edmundsbury and Ipswich, had *'startled his flock by insisting that the Christmas message should include secret police, the massacre of children by troops and contemplation of the baby Jesus as a refugee and asylum seeker'*. Since the biblical texts do, of course, describe exactly these facts, there's no 'should' about it, and if the good Christians of the Bishop's flock were startled by any of this, it does make you wonder exactly what Bible they had been reading. But I suspect the startled person was really the reporter! ...

Kathy Galloway, from *Going Home Another Way*

December

December 26

St Stephen's Day

... Indeed the Greek word for witness, *marturos*, gives us the term martyrdom, which ... was central to the Irish monastic culture in which Columba was brought up. Being a martyr does not necessarily mean, just as it did not mean for Columba and his contemporaries, facing persecution and dying for the faith. It does mean constant witness to Christ through life and example. It also means simply being around, as Jesus was, to listen and pray with people, to stand alongside them in their brokenness and to help them to wholeness. This unspectacular if intensely demanding and draining ministry of presence may well be one of the most important ways in which the church can serve God and his people today when so many other specialist agencies and professional carers are available only by appointment during office hours.

Ian Bradley, from *Columba: Pilgrim and Penitent*

December 27

O Pilgrim God,
abandoning that which is no longer needed:
Come with us on our journey;
show us how to travel lightly,
keeping only what we need to grow.

Ruth Burgess, from *Hear my Cry*

December 28

Holy Innocents Day

Cursed be the work
that maims children
and destroys parents
and lays bare the land.
And when we forget
the cost of our prosperity
disturb us till we understand
... and change.

Ruth Burgess, from *Praying for the Dawn*

December 29

Within the Irish monastic tradition penitence provided a pastorally sensitive way of dealing with the real human problems of sin, guilt and alienation. It was more of an approach and an attitude of mind than a system or mechanism. At its heart was the understanding that forgiveness is available over and over and that both penitent and priest are pilgrims and soul friends together in a similar condition of brokenness.

Ian Bradley, from *Columba:Pilgrim and Penitent*

December

December 30

Lord Jesus:
it is wonderful to know of Your incarnation
that You really came in the flesh,
have walked where we walk,
have felt what we feel:
and that time and time again You could not get away to pray
because of the pressures of everyday.
It is so wonderful to know that You came that we might find you
in the pressure of life.

George MacLeod, from *The Whole Earth Shall Cry Glory*

December 31

In work and worship
GOD IS WITH US
Gathered and scattered
GOD IS WITH US
Now and always
GOD IS WITH US

Responses from the Iona Community's daily 'office', from *Bread for the Road*

Sources

50 Great Prayers from the Iona Community, Neil Paynter (ed.), 2011
50 New Prayers from the Iona Community, Neil Paynter (ed.), 2012
A Blessing to Follow: Contemporary Parables for Living, Tom Gordon, 2009
A Book of Blessings: And How To Write Your Own, Ruth Burgess, 2001
'A Framework for a Memorial Event', Tom Gordon, 2011 (download)
A Heart Broken Open: Radical Faith in an Age of Fear, Ray Gaston, 2009
A Heart for Creation: Worship Resources and Reflections on the Environment, Chris Polhill, 2010
A Heart on Fire: Living as a Mystic in Today's World, Annika Spalde, 2010
A Need For Living: Signposts on the Journey of Life and Beyond, Tom Gordon, 2001
A Storehouse of Kingdom Things: Resources for the Faith Journey, Ian M. Fraser, 2010
A Telling Place: Reflections on Stories of Women in the Bible, Joy Mead, 2002
A Way of Knowing, Joy Mead, 2012
A Wee Worship Book, Wild Goose Worship Group, 1999
Acorns and Archangels: Resources for Ordinary Time – Feast of the Transfiguration to All Hallows', Ruth Burgess, 2009
Advent Readings from Iona, Jan Sutch Pickard and Brian Woodcock, 2000
All That Matters: Collected Scripts from Radio 2's 'Thought for the Day', John L. Bell, 2012
Around a Thin Place: An Iona Pilgrimage Guide, Jane Bentley and Neil Paynter, 2011
Bare Feet and Buttercups: Resources for Ordinary Time – Trinity Sunday to the Feast of the Transfiguration, Ruth Burgess, 2008
'Be still and know that I am God', by Annie Heppenstall, 2011 (download)
Between High and Low Water: Sojourner Songs, Jan Sutch Pickard, 2008
Blessed Be Our Table: Graces for Mealtimes and Reflections on Food, Neil Paynter, 2003
Bread for the Road: A Month of Daily Readings from Coracle, Neil Paynter (ed.) (download), 2010
Bridging the Gap: Has the Church Failed the Poor?, John Harvey, republished by Wild Goose Publications, 2008
Candles & Conifers: Resources for All Saints' and Advent, Ruth Burgess, 2005
Chasing the Wild Goose: the Story of the Iona Community, Ron Ferguson, republished by Wild Goose Publications, 1998
Cherish the Earth: Reflections on a Living Planet, Mary Low, 2003

Christ of the Celts: The Healing of Creation, Philip Newell, 2008

Columba: Pilgrim and Penitent, Ian Bradley, 1996

Coming In: Gays and Lesbians Reclaiming the Spiritual Journey, Urs Mattman, 2006

Daily Readings with George MacLeod, Ron Ferguson (ed.), republished by Wild Goose Publications, 2001

Dandelions and Thistles: Biblical Meditations from the Iona Community, Jan Sutch Pickard, 2001

Dirt, Mess and Danger: Liturgies and Worship Resources, Glendon Macaulay, 2011

Disturbing Complacency: Preparing for Christmas, Lisa Bodenheim, 2007

Doing December Differently: An Alternative Christmas Handbook, 2006, Rosie Miles and Nicola Slee

Down to Earth: Stories and Sketches, Neil Paynter, 2009

Each Day & Each Night: Celtic Prayers from Iona, Philip Newell, 1994

Eggs and Ashes: Practical and Liturgical Resources for Lent and Holy Week, Ruth Burgess and Chris Polhill, 2001

Every Creature a Word of God: Compassion for Animals as Christian Spirituality, Annika Spalde and Pelle Strindlund, 2008 (download)

Exile in Israel: A Personal Journey with the Palestinians, Runa Mackay, 1995

Fire and Bread: Resources for Easter Day to Trinity Sunday, Ruth Burgess, 2003

For God's Sake ... Unity: An Ecumenical Voyage with the Iona Community, Maxwell Craig, 1998

Friends and Enemies: A Book of Short Prayers and Some Ways to Write Your Own, Ruth Burgess, 2001

Gathered and Scattered: Readings and Meditations from the Iona Community, Neil Paynter (ed.), 2007

George MacLeod: A Biography, Ron Ferguson, republished by Wild Goose Publications, 2001

Gobsmacked: Daily Devotions for Advent, Thom Shuman, 2011

God in the Dark: Rebuilding Faith When Bad Stuff Happens, Peter Longson, 2012

Going Home Another Way: Daily Readings and Resources for Christmastide, Neil Paynter (ed.), 2008

Good News of Great Joy: Daily Readings for Advent from Around the World, Peter Millar and Neil Paynter (ed.), 2010

Growing Hope: Daily Readings, Neil Paynter (ed.), 2006

Growing Up With God: Using Stories to Explore a Child's Faith and Life, Nancy Cocks, 2003

Hard Words for Interesting Times: Biblical Texts in Contemporary Contexts, John L. Bell, 2003

Hay & Stardust: Resources for Christmas to Candlemas, Ruth Burgess, 2005

Hear My Cry: A Daily Prayer Book for Advent, Ruth Burgess, 2005

Holy Ground: Liturgies and Worship Resources for an Engaged Spirituality, Helen Boothroyd and Neil Paynter, 2005

Invocations: Calling on the God in All, Richard Skinner, 2005

Iona Abbey Music Book, Iona Community, 2003

Iona Abbey Worship Book, Iona Community, 2001

Iona Dawn: Through Holy Week with the Iona Community, Neil Paynter (ed.), 2006

Iona God's Energy: the Spirituality and Vision of the Iona Community, Norman Shanks, republished by Wild Goose, 2009

Iona: Images and Reflections, Neil Paynter and David Coleman, 2007

It Doesn't Have to Be Like This: Global Economics – a New Way Forward, Margaret Legum, 2002

Labyrinth: Landscape of the Soul, Di Williams, 2009

Lent and Easter Readings from Iona, Neil Paynter (ed.), 2001

Living by the Rule: the Rule of the Iona Community, Kathy Galloway, 2010

Living Letters of the Word: Readings and Meditations from the Iona Community, Neil Paynter (ed.), 2012

'Love Wastefully and Save the World: A Liturgy for Monday of Holy Week', Sally Foster-Fulton, 2012 (download)

Making Peace in Practice and Poetry, Joy Mead, 2003

Meditations from the Iona Community, Iain Reid, 1998

Moon Under Her Feet: Women of the Apocalypse, Kim S. Vidal, 2004. Original edition published by the Pilgrim Press.

New Journeys Now Begin: Learning on the Path of Grief and Loss, Tom Gordon, 2006

No Ordinary Child: A Christian Mother's Acceptance of Her Gay Son, Jacqueline Ley, 2001

Our Hearts Still Sing: A Book of Readings and Reflections, Peter Millar, 2004

Out of Iona: Words from a Crossroads of the World, Jan Sutch Pickard, 2003

Outside the Safe Place: An Oral History of the Early Years of the Iona Community, Anne Muir, 2011

Pathways for Pilgrims: Discovering the Spirituality of the Iona Community in 28 Days, Chris King, 2012

Pearls of Life: For the Personal Spiritual Journey, Martin Lönnebo, Carolina Welin,

Carolina Johnasson, 2007. English translation © 2006 Augsburg Fortress

Pilgrim's Guide to Iona Abbey, Chris Polhill, 2006

Practising the Sacred Art of Listening: A Guide to Enrich Your Relationships & Kindle Your Spiritual Life, Kay Lindahl, 2003

Praying with Our Hands: 21 Practices of Embodied Prayer from the World's Spiritual Traditions, Jon M. Sweeney, 2001. Original edition published in the United States by SkyLight Paths © 2000 SkyLight Paths Publishing

Pushing the Boat Out: New Poetry, Kathy Galloway (ed.), 1995

Radical Hospitality: Benedict's Way of Love, Daniel Homan o.s.b and Lonni Collins Pratt, 2007. Original edition published in the United States by Paraclete Press.

Reclaiming the Sealskin: Meditations in the Celtic Spirit, Annie Heppenstall, 2002

Return Blessings: Ecofeminist Liturgies Healing the Earth, Diann L. Neu, 2004. Published in the United States by Pilgrim Press, 2002

St Cuthbert's Way: A Pilgrims' Companion, Mary Low, 2000

Tell Me the Stories of Jesus: A Companion to the Remembered Bible, Janet Lees, 2011

The Dream of Learning Our True Name, Kathy Galloway, 2004

The Earth Under Threat: A Christian Perspective, Ghillean Prance, 1996

The Fire Within: Sermons form the Edge of Exile, Allan Boesak, 2004. First published by the New World Foundation, South Africa, 2004

The Green Heart of the Snowdrop, Kate McIlhagga, 2004

The Healer's Tree: A Bible-based Resource of Ecology, Peace and Justice, Annie Heppenstall, 2001

The Jesse Tree: Daily Readings for Advent, Thom Shuman, 2005

The One Loaf: An Everyday Celebration, Joy Mead, 2000

The Pattern of Our Days: Liturgies and Resources for Worship from the Iona Community, Kathy Galloway (ed.), 1998

The Sacred Art of Listening: Forty Reflections for Cultivating a Spiritual Practice, Kay Lindahl, 2002

The Tenderness of Conscience: African Renaissance and the Spirituality of Politics, Allan Boesak, 2008. First edition published by Sun Press, South Africa, 2005

The Way Ahead: Grown-up Christians, Ian M Fraser, 2006

The Whole Earth Shall Cry Glory: Iona Prayers, George MacLeod, 1985

This Is the Day: Readings and Meditations from the Iona Community, Neil Paynter (ed.), 2002

Through Wood: Prayers and Poems Reconnecting with the Forest, Alison Swinfen, 2009

We Journey in Hope: Reflections on the Words from the Cross, Neil Paynter (ed.), 2011
Welcoming Each Wonder: More Contemporary Stories for Reflection, Tom Gordon, 2010
Where Are the Altars?, Joy Mead, 2007
Wild Goose Chase: Exploring the Spirituality of Everyday life, Annie Heppenstall, 2006
With An Open Eye: Parables with Meaning for Today, Tom Gordon, 2011
Word of Mouth: Using the Remembered bible for Building Community, Janet Lees, 2007
Words and Wonderings: Conversations with Present-day Prophets, Joy Mead, 2011

Pieces © individual authors
All books and downloads available from Wild Goose Publications:
www.ionabooks.com

Wild Goose Publications, the publishing house of the Iona Community established in the Celtic Christian tradition of Saint Columba, produces books, e-books, CDs and digital downloads on:

- holistic spirituality
- social justice
- political and peace issues
- healing
- innovative approaches to worship
- song in worship, including the work of the Wild Goose Resource Group
- material for meditation and reflection

For more information:

Wild Goose Publications
Fourth Floor, Savoy House
140 Sauchiehall Street,
Glasgow G2 3DH, UK

Tel. +44 (0)141 332 6292
Fax +44 (0)141 332 1090
e-mail: admin@ionabooks.com

or visit our website at
www.ionabooks.com
for details of all our products and online sales